INTRODUCTION to
MARX, ENGELS, MARXISM

by V.I. LENIN

INTERNATIONAL PUBLISHERS
New York

Library of Congress Cataloging-in-Publication Data

Lenin, Vladimir Il'ich, 1870-1924
    Introduction to Marx, Engels, Marxism

    1. Marx, Karl, 1818-1883   2. Engels, Friedrich,
1820-1895.   3. Communism.   4. Communism-Soviet Union
5. Kommunisticheskaia partiia Sovetskogo Soiuza.
6. Trade-unions--Europe.   1. Title
HX39.5.L4424   1986   335.4   86-21012

ISBN10: 0-7178-0647-2
ISBN13: 978-0-7178-0647-8

This printing, 2016

INTRODUCTION to MARX, ENGELS, MARXISM

Editor's Note

A number of famous articles by Lenin and a few selected excerpts from his works dealing with the historical approach and evolution of Marxism are presented in chronological order in this brief anthology.

A major portion of this book consists of the essay on Karl Marx and his teachings which Lenin wrote for a Russian encyclopedia. He began writing the essay in July 1914 while in Galicia, before the outbreak of World War I, and finished it in Switzerland in November of the same year. It was printed in an abridged form in Vol. xxvii of the *Granat Encyclopedia* (1915) under the heading "Marx," together with a bibliography prepared by Lenin as an annex.

However, two sections of Lenin's essay were omitted, one headed "Socialism" and the other "Tactics of the Class Struggle of the Proletariat." In addition, there were other omissions and changes of an editorial nature, including those required by the Tsarist censorship. In the present edition the full text of Lenin's manuscript is reproduced, with the exception of the bibliographical annex, which now would be of limited interest to the general reader. Instead, books and other writings cited by Lenin and available in English editions are given in the reference notes.

Together, the selections in this brief anthology serve as a brief introduction to the rich heritage of Marxism. They begin with Lenin's essay on Engels, written shortly after Engels' death in 1895.

Contents

1. FREDERICK ENGELS[1]

Oh, what a lamp of reason ceased to burn,
Oh, what a heart then ceased to throb![2]

On August 5, 1895, Frederick Engels died in London. After his friend Karl Marx (who died in 1883), Engels was the most noteworthy scholar and teacher of the modern proletariat in all the civilized world. From the time that fate brought Karl Marx and Frederick Engels together, the life work of each of the two friends became the common cause of both. And so, to understand what Frederick Engels has done for the proletariat, one must have a clear idea of the significance of Marx's work and teaching for the development of the contemporary labor movement. Marx and Engels were the first to show that the working class and the demands of the working class are a necessary outcome of the present economic system, which together with the bourgeoisie inevitably creates and organizes the proletariat. They showed that it is not the well-meaning efforts of noble-minded individuals, but the class struggle of the organized proletariat that will deliver humanity from the evils which now oppress it. In their scientific works, Marx and Engels were the first to explain that socialism is not the invention of dreamers, but the final aim and inevitable result of the development of the productive forces of modern society. All recorded history hitherto has been a history of class struggle, of the succession of the rule and victory of certain social classes over others. And this will continue until the foundations of class struggle and of class rule—private property and anarchic social production—disappear. The interests of the proletariat demand the destruction of these foundations, and therefore the conscious class struggle of the organized workers must be directed against them. And every class struggle is a political struggle.

These views of Marx and Engels have now been adopted by all proletarians who are fighting for their emancipation. But when in the forties the two friends took part in the socialist literature and social movements of their time, such opinions were absolutely novel. At that time there were many people, talented and untalented, honest and dishonest, who, while absorbed in the struggle for political freedom, in the struggle against the despotism of monarchs, police and priests, failed to observe the antagonism between the interests of the bourgeoisie and the interests of the proletariat. These people would not even admit the idea that the workers should act as an independent social force. On the other hand, there were many dreamers, some of them geniuses, who thought that it was only necessary to convince the rulers and the governing classes of the injustice of the contemporary social order, and it would then be easy to establish peace and general well-being on earth. They dreamt of socialism without a struggle. Lastly, nearly all the Socialists of that time and the friends of the working class generally regarded the proletariat only as an *ulcer*, and observed with horror how this ulcer grew with the growth of industry. They all, therefore, were intent on how to stop the development of industry and of the proletariat, how to stop the "wheel of history." Far from sharing the general fear of the development of the proletariat, Marx and Engels placed all their hopes on the continued growth of the proletariat. The greater the number of proletarians, the greater would be their power as a revolutionary class, and the nearer and more possible would socialism become. The services rendered by Marx and Engels to the working class may be expressed in a few words thus: they taught the working class to know itself and be conscious of itself, and they substituted science for dreams.

That is why the name and life of Engels should be known to every worker. That is why in this collection of articles,[3] the aim of which, as of all our publications, is to awaken class consciousness in the Russian workers, we must sketch the life and work of Frederick Engels, one of the two great teachers of the modern proletariat.

Engels was born in 1820 in Barmen, in the Rhine province of the kindgom of Prussia. His father was a manufacturer. In 1838, Engels, without having completed his studies at the gymnasium, was forced by family circumstances to enter one of the commercial houses of Bremen as a clerk. Commercial affairs did not prevent Engels from pursuing his scientific and political education. He came to hate autocracy and the tyranny of bureaucrats while still at the gymnasium. The study of philosophy led him further. At that time Hegel's teaching dominated German philosophy, and Engels became his follower. Although Hegel himself was an admirer of the autocratic Prussian state, in whose service he stood as a professor in the University of Berlin, Hegel's *teaching* was revolutionary. Hegel's faith in human reason and its rights, and the fundamental thesis of the Hegelian philosophy, namely, that the universe is subject to a constant process of change and development, was leading those of the disciples of the Berlin philosopher who refused to reconcile themselves to the existing state of affairs to the idea that the struggle against this state of affairs, the struggle against existing wrong and prevalent evil, is also rooted in the universal law of eternal development. If all things develop, if institutions keep giving place to other institutions, why should the autocracy of the Prussian king or of the Russian tsar, why should the enrichment of an insignificant minority at the expense of the vast majority, or the domination of the bourgeoisie over the people, continue forever? Hegel's philosophy spoke of the development of the mind and of ideas; it was *idealistic*. From the development of the mind it deduced the development of nature, of man, and of human, social relations. Retaining Hegel's idea of the eternal process of development,* Marx and Engels rejected the preconceived idealist view; turning to the facts of life, they saw that it was not the development of mind that explained the development of nature but that, on the contrary, the explanation of mind must be derived from nature, from matter. . . . Unlike Hegel and the other Hegelians, Marx and Engels were materialists. Regarding the world and humanity materialistically, they perceived that just as material causes lie at the basis of all the phenomena of nature, so the development of human society is condi-

---

*Marx and Engels frequently pointed out that in their intellectual development they were very much indebted to the great German philosophers, particularly to Hegel. "Without German philosophy," Engels says, "there would have been no scientific socialism."[4]

tioned by the development of material, productive forces. On the development of productive forces depend the relations which men enter into one with another in the production of the things required for the satisfaction of human needs. And in these relations lies the explanation of all the phenomena of social life, human aspirations, ideas and laws. The development of productive forces creates social relations based upon private property, but now we see that this same development of the productive forces deprives the majority of their property and concentrates it in the hands of an insignificant minority. It destroys property, the basis of the modern social order, it itself strives towards the very aim which the Socialists have set themselves. All the Socialists have to do is to realize which of the social forces, owing to its position in modern society, is interested in bringing about socialism, and to impart to this force the consciousness of its interests and of its historical mission. This force is the proletariat. Engels got to know it in England, in the center of British industry, Manchester, where he settled in 1842, entering the service of a commercial house of which his father was a shareholder. Here Engels did not merely sit in the factory office but wandered about the slums where the workers were cooped up. He saw their poverty and misery with his own eyes. But he did not confine himself to personal observations. He read all that had been revealed before him on the condition of the British working class and carefully studied all the official documents he could lay his hands on. The fruit of these studies and observations was the book which appeared in 1845: *The Condition of the Working Class in England*. We have already mentioned the chief service rendered by Engels as the author of *The Condition of the Working Class in England*. Many even before Engels had described the sufferings of the proletariat and had pointed to the necessity of helping it. Engels was the *first* to say that *not only* was the proletariat a suffering class, but that, in fact, the disgraceful economic condition of the proletariat was driving it irresistibly forward and compelling it to fight for its ultimate emancipation. And the fighting proletariat *would help itself.* The political movement of the working class would inevitably lead the workers to realize that their only salvation lay in socialism. On the other hand, socialism would become a force only when it became the aim of the *political* struggle of the working *class.* Such are the main ideas of Engel's book on the condition of the working class in England, ideas that have now been adopted by all thinking and fighting proletarians, but which at that time were entirely new. These ideas were enunciated in his book, written in an absorbing style and filled with most authentic and shocking pictures of the misery of the English proletariat. This book was a terrible indictment of capitalism and the bourgeoisie. It created a very profound impression. Engels's book began to be quoted everywhere as presenting the best picture of the condition of the modern proletariat. And, in fact, neither before 1845 nor after has there appeared so striking and truthful a picture of the misery of the working class.

It was not until he came to England that Engels became a Socialist. In Manchester he formed contacts with people active in the British labor movement at the time and began to write for English socialist publications. In 1844, while on his way back to Germany, he became acquainted in Paris with Marx, with whom he had already started a correspondence. In Paris, under the influence of the French Socialists and French life, Marx had also become a Socialist. Here the friends jointly wrote a book entitled *The Holy Family, or Critique of Critical Critique*. This book, which appeared a year before *The Condition of the Working Class in England*, and the greater part of which was written by Marx, contains the foundations of revolutionary materialist socialism, the main ideas of which we have expounded above. *The Holy Family* is a facetious nickname for the Bauer brothers, philosophers, and their followers. These gentlemen preached a criticism which stood above all reality, which stood above parties and politics, which rejected all practical activity, and which only "critically" contemplated the surrounding world and the events going on within it. These gentlemen, the Bauers, superciliously regarded the proletariat as an uncritical mass. Marx and Engels vigorously opposed this absurd and harmful trend. On behalf of a real human personality—the worker, trampled down by the ruling classes and the state—they demanded, not contemplation, but a struggle for a better order of society. They, of course, regarded the proletariat as the power that was capable of waging this struggle and that was interested in it. Even before the appearance of *The Holy Family*, Engels had published in Marx's and Ruge's *Deutsch-Französische Jahrbücher*[5] the "Critical Essays on Political Economy," in which he examined the principal phenomena of the contemporary economic order from a socialist standpoint and concluded that they were necessary consequences of the rule of private property. Intercourse with Engels was undoubtedly a factor in Marx's decision to study political economy, a science in which his works have produced a veritable revolution.

From 1845 to 1847 Engels lived in Brussels and Paris, combining scientific pursuits with practical activities among the German workers in Brussels and

Paris. Here Marx and Engels formed contact with the secret German Communist League, which commissioned them to expound the main principles of the socialism they had worked out. Thus arose the famous *Manifesto of the Communist Party* of Marx and Engels, published in 1848. This little booklet is worth whole volumes: to this day its spirit inspires and motivates the organized and fighting proletariat of the entire civilized world.

The revolution of 1848, which broke out first in France and then spread to other countries of Western Europe, brought Marx and Engels back to their native country. Here, in Rhenish Prussia, they took charge of the democratic *Neue Rheinische Zeitung* published in Cologne. The two friends were the heart and soul of all revolutionary-democratic aspirations in Rhenish Prussia. They defended the interests of the people and of freedom against the reactionary forces to the last ditch. The reactionary forces, as we know, gained the upper hand. The *Neue Rheinische Zeitung* was suppressed. Marx, who during his exile had lost his Prussian citizenship, was deported; Engels took part in the armed popular uprising, fought for liberty in three battles, and after the defeat of the rebels fled, via Switzerland, to London.

There Marx also settled. Engels soon became a clerk once more, and later a shareholder, in the Manchester commercial house in which he had worked in the forties. Until 1870 he lived in Manchester, while Marx lived in London, which, however, did not prevent them maintaining a most lively intellectual intercourse: they corresponded almost daily. In this correspondence the two friends exchanged views and knowledge and continued to collaborate in the working out of scientific socialism. In 1870 Engels moved to London, and their common intellectual life, full of strenuous labor, continued until 1883, when Marx died. Its fruit was, on Marx's side, *Capital*, the greatest work on political economy of our age, and on Engels's side—a number of works, large and small. Marx worked on the analysis of the complex phenomena of capitalist economy. Engels, in simply written and frequently polemical works, dealt with the more general scientific problems and with diverse phenomena of the past and present in the spirit of the materialist conception of history and Marx's economic theory. Of these works of Engels we shall mention: the polemical work against Dühring (in which are analyzed highly important problems in the domain of philosophy, natural science and the social sciences),* *The Origin of the Family, Private Property and the State* (translated into Russian, published in St. Petersburg, 3rd ed., 1895). *Ludwig Feuerbach* (Russian translation with notes by G. Plekhanov, Geneva, 1892), an article on the foreign policy of the Russian government (translated into Russian in the Geneva *Sotsial-Demokrat*, Nos. 1 and 2),[7] remarkable articles on the housing question,[8] and finally, two small but very valuable articles on the economic development of Russia (*Frederick Engels on Russia*, translated into Russian by Vera Zasulich, Geneva, 1894).[9] Marx died before he could complete his vast work on capital. In the rough, however, it was already finished, and after the death of his friend, Engels undertook the onerous labor of preparing and publishing the second and third volumes of *Capital*. He published Volume II in 1885

---

*This is a wonderfully rich and instructive book.[6] Unfortunately, only a small portion of it, containing a historical outline of the development of socialism, has been translated into Russian. (*The Development of Scientific Socialism*, 2nd ed., Geneva, 1892.)

and Volume III in 1894, (his death prevented the prepartion of Volume IV).[10] These two volumes entailed a vast amount of labor. Adler, the Austrian Social-Democrat, has rightly remarked that by publishing Volumes II and III of *Capital* Engels erected a majestic monument to the genius who had been his friend, a monument on which, without intending it, he indelibly carved his own name. And, indeed, these two volumes of *Capital* are the work of two men: Marx and Engels. Ancient stories contain many moving instances of friendship. The European proletariat may say that its science was created by two scholars and fighters, whose relations to each other surpassed the most moving stories of human friendship among the ancients. Engels always—and, on the whole, justly—placed himself after Marx. "In Marx's lifetime," he wrote to an old friend, "I played second fiddle."[11] His love for the living Marx, and his reverence for the memory of the dead Marx were limitless. In this stern fighter and strict thinker beat a deeply loving heart.

After the movement of 1848-49, Marx and Engels in exile did not occupy themselves with science alone. In 1864 Marx founded the International Workingmen's Association, and led this society for a whole decade. Engels also took an active part in its affairs. The work of the International Association, which, in accordance with Marx's idea, united proletarians of all countries, was of tremendous significance in the development of the working-class movement. But even after the International Association came to an end in the seventies the unifying role of Marx and Engels did not cease. On the contrary, it may be said that their importance as spiritual leaders of the labor movement steadily grew, inasmuch as the movement itself grew uninterruptedly. After the death of Marx, Engels continued alone to be the counsellor and leader of the European Socialists. His advice and directions were sought for equally by the German Socialists, who, despite government persecution, grew rapidly and steadily in strength, and by representatives of backward countries, such as Spaniards, Rumanians and Russians, who were obliged to ponder over and weigh their first steps. They all drew on the rich store of knowledge and experience of old Engels.

Marx and Engels, who both knew Russian and read Russian books, took a lively interest in Russia, followed the Russian revolutionary movement with sympathy and maintained contact with Russian revolutionaries. They were both *democrats* before they became Socialists, and the democratic feeling of *hatred* for political despotism was exceedingly strong in them. This direct political feeling, combined with a profound theoretical understanding of the connection between political despotism and economic oppression, as well as their rich experience of life, made Marx and Engels uncommonly responsive precisely from the *political* standpoint. That is why the heroic struggle of the handful of Russian revolutionaries against the mighty tsarist government evoked a most sympathetic echo in the hearts of these tried revolutionaries. On the other hand, the tendency to turn away from the most immediate and important task of the Russian Socialists, namely, the conquest of political freedom, for the sake of illusory economic advantages, naturally appeared suspicious in their eyes and was even regarded by them as a direct betrayal of the great cause of the social revolution. "The emancipation of the proletariat must be the work of the proletariat itself"— Marx and Engels constantly taught. But in order to fight for its economic emancipation, the proletariat must win for itself certain *political* rights. Moreover, Marx and Engels clearly saw that a political revolution in Russia would be of tremendous significance to the West European labor movement as well. Autocratic Russia had always been a bulwark of European reaction in general. The extraordinarily favorable international position enjoyed by Russia as a result of the war of 1870, which for a long time sowed discord between Germany and France, of course only enhanced the importance of autocratic Russia as a reactionary force. Only a free Russia, a Russia that had no need either to oppress the Poles, Finns, Germans, Armenians or any other small nations, or constantly to incite France and Germany against each other, would enable modern Europe to free itself from the burden of war, would weaken all the reactionary elements in Europe and would increase the power of the European working class. Engels therefore ardently desired the establishment of political freedom in Russia for the sake of the progress of the labor movement in the West as well. In him the Russian revolutionaries have lost their best friend.

May the memory of Frederick Engels, the great champion and teacher of the proletariat, live for ever!

Autumn, 1895

First published in the symposium *Rabotnik*, Nos. 1–2, 1896
English edition, Lenin, *Collected Works* 2:15–27

2. OUR PROGRAM[1]

International Social-Democracy is at present in a state of ideological wavering. Hitherto the doctrines of Marx and Engels were considered to be the firm foundation of revolutionary theory, but voices are now being raised everywhere to proclaim these doctrines inadequate and obsolete. Whoever declares himself to be a Social-Democrat and intends to publish a Social-Democratic organ must define precisely his attitude to a question that is preoccupying the attention of the German Social-Democrats and not of them alone.

We take our stand entirely on the Marxist theoretical position: Marxism was the first to transform socialism from a utopia into a science, to lay a firm foundation for this science, and to indicate the path that must be followed in further developing and elaborating it in all its parts. It disclosed the nature of modern capitalist economy by explaining how the hire of the laborer, the purchase of labor power, conceals the enslavement of millions of propertyless people by a handful of capitalists, the owners of the land, factories, mines, and so forth. It showed that all modern capitalist development displays the tendency of large-scale production to eliminate petty production and creates conditions that make a socialist system of society possible and necessary. It taught us how to discern, beneath the pall of rooted customs, political intrigues, abstruse laws, and intricate doctrines—the *class struggle*, the struggle between the propertied classes in all their variety and the propertyless mass, the *proletariat*, which is at the head of all the propertyless. It made clear the real task of a revolutionary socialist party: not to draw up plans for refashioning society, not to preach to the capitalists and their hangers-on about improving the lot of the workers, not to hatch conspiracies, *but to organize the class struggle of the proletariat and to lead this struggle, the ultimate aim of which is the conquest of political power by the proletariat and the organization of a socialist society.*

And we now ask: Has anything new been introduced into this theory by its loud-voiced "renovators" who are raising so much noise in our day and have grouped themselves around the German socialist Bernstein? *Absolutely nothing.* Not by a single step have they advanced the science which Marx and Engels enjoined us to develop; they have not taught the proletariat any new methods of struggle; they have only retreated, borrowing fragments of backward theories and preaching to the proletariat, not the theory of struggle, but the theory of concession—concession to the most vicious enemies of the proletariat, the governments and bourgeois parties who never tire of seeking new means of baiting the socialists. Plekhanov, one of the founders and leaders of Russian Social-Democracy, was entirely right in ruthlessly criticising Bernstein's latest "critique"[2]; the views of Bernstein have now been rejected by the representatives of the German workers as well (at the Hannover Congress).[3]

We anticipate a flood of accusations for these words; the shouts will rise that we want to convert the socialist party into an order of "true believers" that persecutes "heretics" for deviations from "dogma," for every independent opinion, and so forth. We know about all these fashionable and trenchant phrases. Only there is not a grain of truth or sense in them. There can be no strong socialist party without a revolutionary theory that unites all socialists, from which they draw all their convictions, and that they apply in their methods of struggle and means of action. To defend such a theory, which to the best of your knowledge you consider to be true, against unfounded attacks and attempts to corrupt it is not to imply that you are an enemy of *all* criticism. We do not regard Marx's theory as something completed and inviolable; on the contrary, we are convinced that it has only laid the foundation stone of the science which socialists *must* develop in all directions if they wish to keep pace with life. We think that an *independent* elaboration of Marx's theory is especially essential for Russian socialists; for this theory provides only general *guiding* principles, which, *in particular*, are applied in England differently than in France, in France differently than in Germany, and in Germany differently than in Russia. We shall therefore gladly afford space in our paper for articles on theoretical questions and we invite all comrades openly to discuss controversial points.

What are the main questions that arise in the application to Russia of the program common to all Social-Democrats? We have stated that the essence of this program is to organize the class struggle of the proletariat and to lead this struggle, the ultimate aim of which is the conquest of political power by the proletariat and the establishment of a socialist society. The class struggle of the proletariat comprises the economic struggle (struggle against individual capitalists or against individual groups of capitalists for the improvement of the workers' condition) and the political struggle (struggle against the government for the broadening of the people's rights, i.e., for democracy, and for the broadening of the political power of the proletariat). Some Russian Social-Democrats (among them apparently those who direct *Rabochaya Mysl*)[4] regard the economic struggle as incomparably the more important and almost go so far as to relegate the political struggle to the more or less distant future. This standpoint is utterly false. All Social-Democrats are agreed that it is necessary to organize the economic struggle of the working class, that it is necessary to carry on agitation among the workers on this basis, i.e., to help the workers in their day-to-day struggle against the employers, to draw their attention to every form and every case of oppression and in this way to make clear to them the necessity for combination. But to forget the political struggle for the economic would mean to depart from the basic principle of international Social-Democracy, it would mean to forget what the entire history of the labor movement teaches us. The confirmed adherents of the bourgeoisie and of the government which serves it have even made repeated attempts to organize purely economic unions of workers and to divert them in this way from "politics," from socialism. It is quite possible that the Russian Government, too, may undertake something of the kind, as it has always endeavored to throw some paltry sops or, rather, sham sops, to the people, only to turn their thoughts away from the fact that they are oppressed and without rights. No economic struggle can bring the workers any lasting improvement, or can even be conducted on a large scale, unless the workers have the right freely to organize meetings and unions, to have their own newspapers, and to send their representatives to the national assemblies, as do the workers in Germany and all other European countries (with the exception of Turkey and Russia). But in order to win these rights it is necessary to wage a *political struggle*. In Russia, not only the workers, but all citizens are deprived of political rights. Russia is an absolute and unlimited monarchy. The tsar alone promulgates laws, appoints officials and controls them. For this reason, *it seems* as though in Russia the tsar and the tsarist government are independent of all classes and accord equal treatment to all. But *in reality* all officials are chosen exclusively from the propertied class and all are subject to the influence of the big capitalists, who make the ministers dance to their tune and who achieve whatever they want. The Russian working class is burdened by a double yoke; it is robbed and plundered by the capitalists and the landlords, and to prevent it from fighting them, the police bind it hand and foot, gag it, and every attempt to defend the rights of the people is persecuted. Every strike against a capitalist results in the military and police being let loose on the workers. Every economic struggle necessarily becomes a political struggle, and Social-Democracy must indissolubly combine the one with the other into a *single class struggle of the proletariat*. The first and chief aim of such a struggle must be the conquest of political rights, *the conquest of political liberty*. If the workers of St. Petersburg alone, with a little help from the socialists, have rapidly succeeded in wringing a concession from the government—the adoption of the law on the reduction of the working day[5]—then the Russian working class as a whole, led by a single Russian Social-Democratic Labor Party will be able, in persistent struggle, to win incomparably more important concessions.

The Russian working class is able to wage its economic and political struggle alone, even if no other class comes to its aid. But in the political struggle the workers do not stand alone. The people's complete lack of rights and the savage lawlessness of the bashi-bazouk officials rouse the indignation of all honest educated people who cannot reconcile themselves to the persecution of free thought and free speech; they rouse the indignation of the persecuted Poles, Finns, Jews, and Russian religious sects; they rouse the indignation of the small merchants, manufacturers, and peasants, who can nowhere find protection from the persecution of officials and police. All these groups of the population are incapable, separately, of carrying on a persistent political struggle. But when the working class raises the banner of this struggle, it will receive support from all sides. Russian Social-Democracy will place itself at the head of all fighters for the rights of the people, of all fighters for democracy, and it will prove invincible!

These are our fundamental views, and we shall develop them systematically and from every aspect in our paper. We are convinced that in this way we shall tread the path which has been indicated by the Russian Social-Democratic Labor Party in its published *Manifesto*.[6]

3. ENGELS ON THE IMPORTANCE OF THE THEORETICAL STRUGGLE[1]

Thus, we see that high-sounding phrases against the ossification of thought, etc., conceal unconcern and helplessness with regard to the development of theoretical thought. The case of the Russian Social-Democrats manifestly illustrates the general European phenomenon (long ago noted also by the German Marxists) that the much vaunted freedom of criticism does not imply substitution of one theory for another, but freedom from all integral and pondered theory; it implies eclecticism and lack of principle. Those who have the slightest acquaintance with the actual state of our movement cannot but see that the wide spread of Marxism was accompanied by a certain lowering of the theoretical level. Quite a number of people with very little, and even a total lack of theoretical training joined the movement because of its practical significance and its practical successes. We can judge from that how tactless *Rabocheye Dyelo* is when, with an air of triumph, it quotes Marx's statement: "Every step of real movement is more important than a dozen programs."[2] To repeat these words in a period of theoretical disorder is like wishing mourners at a funeral many happy returns of the day. Moreover, these words of Marx are taken from his letter on the Gotha Programme, in which he *sharply condemns* eclecticism in the formulation of principles. If you must unite, Marx wrote to the party leaders, then enter into agreements to satisfy the practical aims of the movement, but do not allow any bargaining over principles, do not make theoretical "concessions". This was Marx's idea, and yet there are people among us who seek—in his name—to belittle the significance of theory!

Without revolutionary theory there can be no revolutionary movement. This idea cannot be insisted upon too strongly at a time when the fashionable preaching of opportunism goes hand in hand with an infatuation for the narrowest forms of practical activity. Yet, for Russian Social-Democrats the importance of theory is enhanced by three other circumstances, which are often forgotten: first, by the fact that our Party is only in process of formation. Its features are only just becoming defined, and it has as yet far from settled accounts with the other trends of revolutionary thought that threaten to divert the movement from the correct path. On the contrary, precisely the very recent past was marked by a revival of non-Social-Democratic revolutionary trends (an eventuation regarding which Axelrod long ago warned the Economists). Under these circumstances, what at first sight appears to be an "unimportant" error may lead to most deplorable consequences, and only short-sighted people can consider factional disputes and a strict differentiation between shades of opinion inopportune or superfluous. The fate of Russian Social-Democracy for very many years to come may depend on the strengthening of one or the other "shade".

Secondly, the Social-Democratic movement is in its very essence an international movement. This means, not only that we must combat national chauvinism, but that an incipient movement in a young country can be successful only if it makes use of the experiences of other countries. In order to make use of these experiences it is not enough merely to be acquainted with them, or simply to copy out the latest resolutions. What is required is the ability to treat these experiences critically and to test them independently. He who realises how enormously the modern working-class movement has grown and branched out will understand what a reserve of theoretical forces and political (as well as revolutionary) experience is required to carry out this task.

Thirdly, the national tasks of Russian Social-Democracy are such as have never confronted any other socialist party in the world. We shall have occasion further on to deal with the political and organizational duties which the task of emancipating the whole people from the yoke of autocracy imposes upon us. At this point, we wish to state only that the *role of vanguard fighter can be fulfilled only by a party that is guided by the most advanced theory.* To have a concrete understanding of what this means, let the reader recall such predecessors of Russian Social-Democracy as Herzen, Belinsky, Chernyshevsky, and the brilliant galaxy of revolutionaries of the seventies; let him ponder over the world significance which Russian literature is now acquiring; let him . . . but be that enough!

Let us quote what Engels said in 1874 concerning the significance of theory in the Social-Democratic movement. Engels recognizes, *not two* forms of the great struggle of Social-Democracy (political and economic), as is the fashion among us, *but three, placing* *the theoretical struggle on a par with the first two.* His recommendations to the German working-class movement, which had become strong, practically and politically, are so instructive from the standpoint of present-day problems and controversies, that we hope the reader will not be vexed with us for quoting a long passage from his prefatory note to *Der deutsche Bauernkrieg,** which has long become a great bibliographical rarity:

"The German workers have two important advantages over those of the rest of Europe. First, they belong to the most theoretical people of Europe; and they have retained that sense of theory which the so-called 'educated' classes of Germany have almost completely lost. Without German philosophy, which preceded it, particularly that of Hegel, German scientific socialism—the only scientific socialism that has ever existed—would never have come into being. Without a sense of theory among the workers, this scientific socialism would never have entered their flesh and blood as much as is the case. What an immeasurable advantage this is may be seen, on the one hand, from the indifference towards all theory, which is one of the main reasons why the English working-class movement crawls along so slowly in spite of the splendid organization of the individual unions; on the other hand, from the mischief and confusion wrought by Proudhonism, in its original form, among the French and Belgians, and, in the form further caricatured by Bakunin, among the Spaniards and Italians.

---

*Dritter Abdruck. Leipzig, 1875. Verlag der Genossenschaftsbuchdruckerei. (*The Peasant War in Germany.* Third impression. Cooperative Publishers, Leipzig, 1875.—Ed.)

"The second advantage is that, chronologically speaking, the Germans were about the last to come into the workers' movement. Just as German theoretical socialism will never forget that it rests on the shoulders of Saint-Simon, Fourier, and Owen—three men who, in spite of all their fantastic notions and all their utopianism, have their place among the most eminent thinkers of all times, and whose genius anticipated innumerable things, the correctness of which is now being scientifically proved by us—so the practical workers' movement in Germany ought never to forget that it has developed on the shoulders of the English and French movements, that it was able simply to utilize their dearly bought experience, and could now avoid their mistakes, which in their time were mostly unavoidable. Without the precedent of the English trade unions and French workers' political struggles, without the gigantic impulse given especially by the Paris Commune, where would we be now?

"It must be said to the credit of the German workers that they have exploited the advantages of their situation with rare understanding. For the first time since a workers' movement has existed, the struggle is being conducted pursuant to its three sides—the theoretical, the political, and the practical-economic (resistance to the capitalists)—in harmony and in its interconnections, and in a systematic way. It is precisely in this, as it were, concentric attack, that the strength and invincibility of the German movement lies.

"Due to this advantageous situation, on the one hand, and to the insular peculiarities of the English and the forcible suppression of the French movement, on the other, the German workers have for the moment been placed in the vanguard of the proletarian struggle. How long events will allow them to occupy this post of honor cannot be foretold. But let us hope that as long as they occupy it, they will fill it fittingly. This demands redoubled efforts in every field of struggle and agitation. In particular, it will be the duty of the leaders to gain an ever clearer insight into all theoretical questions, to free themselves more and more from the influence of traditional phrases inherited from the old world outlook, and constantly to keep in mind that socialism, since it has become a science, demands that it be pursued as a science, i.e., that it be studied. The task will be to spread with increased zeal among the masses of the workers the ever more clarified understanding thus acquired, to knit together ever more firmly the organization both of the party and of the trade unions. . . .

"If the German workers progress in this way, they will not be marching exactly at the head of the movement—it is not at all in the interest of this movement that the workers of any particular country should march at its head—but they will occupy an honorable place in the battle line; and they will stand armed for battle when either unexpectedly grave trials or momentous events demand of them increased courage, increased determination and energy."[3]

Engels's words proved prophetic. Within a few years the German workers were subjected to unexpectedly grave trials in the form of the Exceptional Law Against the Socialists. And they met those trials armed for battle and succeeded in emerging from them victorious.

The Russian proletariat will have to undergo trials immeasurably graver; it will have to fight a monster compared with which an anti-socialist law in a constitutional country seems but a dwarf. History has now confronted us with an immediate task which is the *most revolutionary* of all the *immediate* tasks confronting the proletariat of any country. The fulfilment of this task, the destruction of the most powerful bulwark, not only of European, but (it may now be said) of Asiatic reaction, would make the Russian proletariat the vanguard of the international revolutionary proletariat. And we have the right to count upon acquiring this honorable title, already earned by our predecessors, the revolutionaries of the seventies, if we succeed in inspiring our movement, which is a thousand times broader and deeper, with the same devoted determination and vigor.

4. DIFFERENCES IN THE EUROPEAN LABOR MOVEMENT[1]

The main tactical differences in the modern labor movement in Europe and America may be summed up as the struggle with two main tendencies which depart from Marxism, from the theory that has actually become dominating in this movement. These two tendencies are revisionism (opportunism and reformism) and anarchism (anarcho-syndicalism and anarcho-socialism). Both these deviations from the Marxist theory and tactics which dominate the labor movement are to be observed in various forms and various shades in all civilized countries throughout the history of the mass labor movement of over half a century.

This fact alone makes it clear that these deviations cannot be explained either by accidents, or errors on the part of individuals or groups, or even by the influence of national peculiarities or traditions, etc. There must be some fundamental causes within the economic system itself and in the character of the development of all capitalist countries which constantly breed these deviations. The little book by the

Dutch Marxist, Anton Pannekoek, *The Tactical Differences in the Labour Movement* (*Die taktischen Differenzen in der Arbeiterbewegung*, Hamburg, Erdmann Dubber, 1909), published last year, represents an interesting attempt to explain these causes. We will, in our further exposition, acquaint the reader with the conclusions of Pannekoek, which one cannot help recognizing as quite correct.

One of the deeper causes which give rise to the periodical differences in regard to tactics is the very fact of the growth of the labor movement. If this movement be measured not by the standard of some fantastic ideal, but considered as a practical movement of ordinary people, it will become clear that the continued enrolment of fresh "recruits" and the drawing in of new sections of the toiling masses must inevitably be accompanied by hesitations in theory and tactics, by the repetition of old mistakes and by the temporary return to obsolete views and methods, etc. The labor movement of every country periodically spends more or less of its reserves of energy, attention and time on the "training" of recruits.

Further. The pace of development of capitalism is not the same in various countries and different spheres of national economy. Marxism is more easily, more quickly, more fully and firmly mastered by the working class and its ideologists in conditions of the greatest development of big industry. Economic relations that are backward or fall behind in their development constantly lead to the appearance of adherents of the labor movement who master only certain aspects of Marxism, only separate sections of the new world outlook, only separate slogans and demands, being incapable of breaking decisively with all the traditions of the bourgeois world outlook in general and the bourgeois-democratic world outlook in particular.

Then, a constant source of differences is provided by the dialectic nature of social development which proceeds in contradictions and by means of contradictions. Capitalism is progressive since it destroys the old methods of production and develops the productive forces and at the same time, at a certain stage of development, it delays the growth of these productive forces. It develops, organizes and disciplines the workers; and it presses, oppresses, leads to degeneration, poverty, etc. Capitalism itself creates its own grave-digger, itself creates the elements of the new system and, at the same time, these elements, without a "leap," can change nothing in the general condition of things, cannot touch the domination of capital. Marxism, as a theory of dialectical materialism is capable of embracing these contradictions of actual life, of the history of capitalism and the labor movement. But it is self-evident that the masses learn from life, and not from books, and consequently, individuals and groups constantly exaggerate and raise to a one-sided theory and one-sided system of tactics now one, now another feature of capitalist development, now one, now another "lesson" of this development.

Bourgeois ideologists, liberals and democrats, who do not understand Marxism and the modern labor movement, are constantly jumping from one helpless extreme to another. Now they explain that it is all because wicked persons "incite" class against class, and now they console themselves that the workers' party is a "peaceful party of reform." Both anarcho-syndicalism and reformism must be considered as the direct product of this bourgeois world outlook and influence. They both seize upon *one* side of the labor movement, raise this one-sidedness to a theory and declare as mutually exclusive such tendencies or features of the labor movement as form the specific peculiarity of one or other period, of one or other of the conditions of activity of the working class. But real life and realy history *include* in themselves these various tendencies, just as life and development in nature include in themselves both slow evolution and rapid leaps, breaks in gradualness.

The revisionists consider as phrases all arguments about "leaps" and about the principles underlying the antagonism of the labor movement to the old society. They accept reforms as a partial realization of socialism. The anarcho-syndicalist rejects "petty work," particularly the utilization of the parliamentary tribune. In practice these latter tactics amount to waiting for "big days" and exhibit an inability to gather the forces for creating big events. Both the revisionists and the anarcho-syndicalists hinder the most important and urgent business of uniting the workers in big, strong and well functioning organizations, capable of functioning well under *all* circumstances, imbued with the spirit of the class struggle, clearly recognizing their aims and trained in the real Marxian world outlook.

Here we will permit ourselves a small digression and remark, in parentheses, to avoid possible misunderstanding, that Pannekoek illustrates his analysis *exclusively* by examples from West European history, particularly from Germany and France, and has *absolutely not had* Russia in view. If it sometimes appears that he hints at Russia, this simply is due to the fact that the fundamental tendencies which give rise to definite deviations from Marxist tactics, also manifest themselves with us, notwithstanding the enormous distinction between Russia and the West, in point of culture, modes of life, and historical and economic differences.

Finally, an exceedingly important cause giving rise to differences between members of the labor movement is the changes in the tactics of the ruling classes in general and of the bourgeoisie in particular. If the tactics of the bourgeoisie were always uniform or at least homogeneous, the working class would have quickly learned to reply by equally uniform or homogeneous tactics. The bourgeoisie in all countries in practice inevitably elaborates two systems of governing, two methods of struggle for its interests and for the defense of its domination, and these two methods now replace one another and now interlace in different combinations. These are, first, the method of violence, the method of refusing all concessions to the labor movement, the method of supporting all ancient and dying institutions, the method of uncompromising rejection of reforms. Such is the substance of conservative policy, which is more and more ceasing to be in Western Europe the policy of the landlord classes, and is ever more becoming one of the varieties of general bourgeois policy. The second method is the method of "liberalism," of steps towards the development of political rights, of reforms, of concessions, etc.

The bourgeoisie passes from one method to another not through the malicious design of individuals and not by accident, but by force of the basic contradictoriness of its own position. A normal capitalist society cannot successfully develop without a stabilized representative system, without certain political rights being granted to the population, which is necessarily distinguished by the comparatively high claims it presents with regard to "culture." This demand for a certain minimum of culture arises from the very conditions of the capitalist mode of production with its high technique, complexity, flexibility, mobility, rapidity of development of world competition, etc. In consequence of this, fluctuations in the tactics of the bourgeoisie and transitions from the system of violence to the system of would-be concessions are peculiar to the history of all European countries for the last half century, and various countries mainly develop the application of one or other method at definite periods. For instance, England in the sixties and seventies of the nineteenth century was the classical country of "liberal" bourgeois policy, Germany in the seventies and eighties kept to the method of force, etc.

When this method ruled in Germany, a one-sided echo of this system of bourgeois government was the growth in the labor movement of anarcho-syndicalism, or, as it was then called, anarchism (the "Young"[2] in the beginning of the 'nineties, and Johann Most[3] in the beginning of the 'eighties). When a turn towards "concessions" took place in 1890, this turn proved, as it always has done, even more dangerous for the labor movement, since it gave rise to an equally one-sided echo of bourgeois "reformism": opportunism in the labor movement.

"The positive aim of the liberal progressive policy of the bourgeoisie," says Pannekoek, "is to mislead the workers, to introduce a split in their ranks, to transform their politics into an impotent appendage of an impotent, always impotent and ephemeral, would-be reformism."

The bourgeoisie, not infrequently, attains its object, for a certain time, by means of a "liberal" policy which represents, according to the just remark of Pannekoek, a "more cunning" policy. A part of the workers and a part of their leaders allow themselves to be deceived by seeming concessions. The revisionists proclaim as "obsolete" the doctrine of the class struggle, or begin to carry on a policy which in fact renounces it. The zigzags of bourgeois tactics cause a strengthening of revisionism in the labor movement and not infrequently lead to differences within it to the point of a direct split.

All the causes of the kind indicated evoke differences in relation to the tactics within the labor movement and in the proletarian ranks. But there is not and there cannot be a Chinese wall between the proletariat and the adjacent sections of the petty bourgeoisie, including the peasantry. It is clear that the transition of individuals, groups, and sections of the petty bourgeoisie to the proletariat cannot but give rise, in its turn, to vacillations in the tactics of the latter.

The experience of the labor movement of various countries helps to elucidate the essence of Marxist tactics on concrete practical questions, and helps the younger countries to distinguish more clearly the true class significance of deviations from Marxism and more successfully to fight them.

December 29, 1910.

5. CERTAIN FEATURES OF THE HISTORICAL DEVELOPMENT OF MARXISM

Our doctrine, said Engels—referring to himself and his famous friend—is not a dogma, but a guide to action. This classical statement stresses with remarkable force and expressiveness that aspect of Marxism which is very often lost sight of. And by losing sight of it, we turn Marxism into something one-sided, distorted and lifeless; we deprive it of its life blood; we undermine its basic theoretical foundations—dialectics, the doctrine of historical development, all-embracing and full of contradictions; we undermine its connection with the definite practical tasks of the epoch, which may change with every new turn of history.

Indeed, in our time, among those interested in the fate of Marxism in Russia, we very frequently meet with people who lose sight of just this aspect of Marxism. Yet, it must be clear to everybody that in recent years Russia has undergone changes so abrupt as to alter the situation with unusual rapidity and unusual force—the social and political situation, which in a most direct and immediate manner determines the conditions for action, and hence, its aims. I am not referring, of course, to general and fundamental aims, which do not change with turns of history if the fundamental relation between classes remains unchanged. It is perfectly obvious that this general trend of economic (and not only economic) evolution in Russia, like the fundamental relation between the various classes of Russian society, has not changed during, say, the last six years.

But the aims of immediate and direct action changed very sharply during this period, just as the actual social and political situation changed, and *consequently*, since Marxism is a living doctrine, *various aspects* of it *were bound* to become prominent.

In order to make this idea clear, let us cast a glance at the change in the actual social and political situation over the past six years. We immediately differentiate two three-year periods: one ending roughly with the summer of 1907, and the other with the summer of 1910. The first three-year period, regarded from the purely theoretical standpoint, is distinguished by rapid changes in the fundamental features of the state system in Russia; the course of these changes, moreover, was very uneven and the oscillations in both directions were of considerable amplitude. The social and economic basis of these changes in the "superstructure" was the action of *all* classes of Russian society in *the most diverse* fields (activity inside and outside the Duma, the press, unions, meetings, and so forth), action so open and impressive and on a mass scale such as is rarely to be observed in history.

The second three-year period, on the contrary, is distinguished—we repeat that we confine ourselves to the purely theoretical "sociological" standpoint—by an evolution so slow that it almost amounted to stagnation. There were no changes of any importance to be observed in the state system. There were hardly any open and diversified actions by the *classes* in the majority of the "arenas" in which these actions had developed in the preceding period.

The similarity between the two periods is that Russia underwent capitalist evolution in both of them. The contradiction between this economic evolution and the existence of a number of feudal and medieval institutions still remained and was not stifled, but rather aggravated, by the fact that certain institutions assumed a partially bourgeois character.

The difference between the two periods is that in the first the question of exactly what form the above-mentioned rapid and uneven changes would take was the dominant, history-making issue. The content of these changes was bound to be bourgeois owing to the capitalist character of Russia's evolution; but there are different kinds of bourgeoisie. The middle and big bourgeoisie, which professes a more or less moderate liberalism, was, owing to its very class position, afraid of abrupt changes and strove for the retention of large remnants of the old institutions both in the agrarian system and in the political "superstructure." The rural petty bourgeoisie, interwoven as it is with the peasants who live "solely by the labor of their hands," was bound to strive for bourgeois reforms of a *different* kind, reforms that would leave far less room for medieval survivals. The wage-workers, inasmuch as they consciously realized what was going on around them, were bound to work out for themselves a definite attitude towards this clash of two distinct tendencies. Both tendencies remained within the framework of the bourgeois system, determining entirely different forms of that system, entirely different rates of its development, different degrees of its progressive influence.

Thus, the first period necessarily brought to the fore—and not by chance—those problems of Marxism that are usually referred to as problems of tactics. Nothing is more erroneous than the opinion that the disputes and differences over these questions were disputes among "intellectuals," "a struggle for influence over the immature proletariat," an expression of the "adaptation of the intelligentsia to the proletariat," as *Vekhi*[1] followers of various hues think. On the contrary, it was precisely because this class had reached maturity that it could not remain indifferent to the clash of the two different tendencies in Russia's bourgeois development, and the ideologists of this class could not avoid providing theoretical formulations corresponding (directly or indirectly, in direct or reverse reflection) to these different tendencies.

In the second period the clash between the different tendencies of bourgeois development in Russia was *not* on the order of the day, because *both* these tendencies had been crushed by the "diehards," forced back, driven inwards and, for the time being, stifled. The medieval diehards not only occupied the foreground but also inspired the broadest sections of bourgeois society with the sentiments propagated by *Vekhi*, with a spirit of dejection and recantation. It was not the collision between two methods of reforming the old order that appeared on the surface, but a loss of faith in reforms of any kind, a spirit of "meekness" and "repentance," an enthusiasm for anti-social doctrines, a vogue of mysticism, and so on.

This astonishingly abrupt change was neither accidental nor the result of "external" pressure alone. The preceding period had so profoundly stirred up sections of the population who for generations and centuries had stood aloof from, and had been strangers to, political issues that it was natural and inevitable that there should emerge "a revaluation of all values," a new study of fundamental problems, a new interest in theory, in elementals, in the ABC of politics. The millions who were suddenly awakened from their long sleep and confronted with extremely important problems could not long remain on this level. They could not continue without a respite, without a return to elementary questions, without a new training which would help them "digest" lessons of unparalleled richness and make it possible for incomparably wider masses again to march forward, but now far more firmly, more consciously, more confidently and more steadfastly.

The dialectics of historical development was such that in the first period it was the attainment of immediate reforms in every sphere of the country's life that was on the order of the day. In the second period it was the critical study of experience, its assimilation by wider sections, its penetration, so to speak, into the subsoil, into the backward ranks of the various classes.

It is precisely because Marxism is not a lifeless dogma, not a completed, ready-made, immutable doctrine, but a living guide to action, that it was bound to reflect the astonishingly abrupt change in the conditions of social life. That change was reflected in profound disintegration and disunity, in every manner of vacillation, in short, in a very serious *internal* crisis of Marxism. Resolute resistance to this disintegration, a resolute and persistent struggle to uphold the *fundamentals* of Marxism, was again placed on the order of the day. In the preceding period, extremely wide sections of the classes that cannot avoid Marxism in formulating their aims had assimilated that doctrine in an extremely one-sided and mutilated fashion. They had learnt by rote certain "slogans," certain answers to tactical questions, *without having understood* the Marxist criteria for these answers. The "revaluation of all values" in the various spheres of social life led to a "revision" of the most abstract and general philosophical fundamentals of Marxism. The influence of bourgeois philosophy in its diverse idealist shades found expression in the Machist[2] epidemic that broke out among the Marxists. The repetition of "slogans" learnt by rote but not understood and not thought out led to the widespread prevalence of empty phrase-mongering. The practical expression of this were such absolutely un-Marxist, petty-bourgeois trends as frank or shamefaced *otzovism*,[3] or the recognition of *otzovism* as a "legal shade" of Marxism.

On the other hand, the spirit of the magazine *Vekhi*, the spirit of renunciation which had taken possession of very wide sections of the bourgeoisie, also permeated the trend wishing to confine Marxist theory and practice to "moderate and careful" channels. All that remained of Marxism here was the phraseology used to clothe arguments about "hierarchy," "hegemony" and so forth, that were thoroughly permeated with the spirit of liberalism.

The purpose of this article is not to examine these arguments. A mere reference to them is sufficient to illustrate what has been said above regarding the depth of the crisis through which Marxism is passing and its connection with the whole social and economic situation in the present period. The questions raised by this crisis cannot be brushed aside. Nothing can be more pernicious or unprincipled than attempts to dismiss them by all phrase-mongering. Nothing is more important than to rally *all* Marxists who have realized the profundity of the crisis and the necessity of combating it, for defense of the theoretical basis of Marxism and its fundamental propositions, that are being distorted from diametrically opposite sides by the spread of bourgeois influence to the various "fellow travelers" of Marxism.

The first three years awakened wide sections to a conscious participation in social life, sections that in many cases are now for the first time beginning to acquaint themselves with Marxism in real earnest. The bourgeoisie press is creating far more fallacious ideas on this score than ever before, and is spreading them more widely. Under these circumstances disintegration in the Marxist ranks is particularly dangerous. Therefore, to understand the reasons for the inevitability of this disintegration at the present time and to close their ranks for consistent struggle against this disintegration is, in the most direct and precise meaning of the term, the task of the day for Marxists.

December 1910

6. THE THREE SOURCES AND THREE COMPONENT PARTS OF MARXISM[1]

Throughout the civilized world the teachings of Marx evoke the utmost hostility and hatred of all bourgeois science (both official and liberal), which regards Marxism as a kind of "pernicious sect." And no other attitude is to be expected, for there can be no "impartial" social science in a society based on class struggle. In one way or another, *all* official and liberal science *defends* wage slavery, where Marxism has declared relentless war on wage slavery. To expect science to be impartial in a wage-slave society is as silly and naive as to expect impartiality from manufacturers on the question of whether workers' wages should be increased by decreasing the profits of capital.

But this is not all. The history of philosophy and the history of social science show with perfect clarity that there is nothing resembling "sectarianism" in Marxism, in the sense of its being a hidebound, petrified doctrine, a doctrine which arose *away from* the highroad of development of world civilization. On the contrary, the genius of Marx consists precisely in the fact that he furnished answers to questions which had already engrossed the foremost minds of humanity. His teachings arose as a direct and immediate *continuation* of the teachings of the greatest representatives of philosophy, political economy and socialism.

The Marxian doctrine is omnipotent because it is true. It is complete and harmonious, and provides men with an integral world conception which is irreconcilable with any form of superstitution, reaction, or defense of bourgeois oppression. It is the legitimate successor of the best that was created by humanity in the nineteenth century in the shape of German philosophy, English political economy and French Socialism.

On these three sources of Marxism, which are at the same time its component parts, we shall dwell briefly.

I

The philosophy of Marxism is *materialism*. Throughout the modern history of Europe, and especially at the end of the eighteenth century in France, which was the scene of a decisive battle against every kind of medieval rubbish, against feudalism in institutions and ideas, materialism has proved to be the only philosophy that is consistent, true to all the teachings of natural science and hostile to superstition, cant and so forth. The enemies of democracy therefore tried in every way to "refute," undermine and defame materialism, and advocated various forms of philosophical idealism, which always, in one way or another, amounts to an advocacy or support of religion.

Marx and Engels always defended philosophical materialism in the most determined manner and repeatedly explained the profound error of every deviation from this basis. Their views are most clearly and fully expounded in the works of Engels, *Ludwig*

Feuerbach and *Anti-Dühring*, which like the *Communist Manifesto*, are handbooks for every class-conscious worker.

But Marx did not stop at the materialism of the eighteenth century; he advanced philosophy. He enriched it with the acquisitions of German classical philosophy, especially of the Hegelian system, which in its turn led to the materialism of Feuerbach. The chief of these acquisitions is *dialectics*, i.e., the doctrine of developments in its fullest and deepest forms, free of one-sidedness—the doctrine of the relativity of human knowledge, which provides us with a reflection of eternally developing matter. The latest discoveries of natural science—radium, electrons, the transmutation of elements—have confirmed remarkably Marx's dialectical materialism, despite the teachings of the bourgeois philosophers with their "new" reversions to old and rotten idealism.

Deepening and developing philosophical materialism, Marx completed it, extended its knowledge of nature to the knowledge of *human society*. Marx's *historical materialism* was one of the greatest achievements of scientific thought. The chaos and arbitrariness that had previously reigned in the views on history and politics gave way to a strikingly integral and harmonious scientific theory,which shows how, in consequence of the growth of productive forces, out of one system of social life another and higher system develops—how capitalism, for instance, grows out of feudalism.

Just as man's knowledge reflects nature (i.e., developing matter), which exists independently of him, so man's *social knowledge* (i.e., the various views and doctrines—philosophical, religious, political, and so forth) reflects the *economic system* of society. Political institutions are a superstructure on the economic foundation. We see, for example, that the various

political forms of the modern European states serve to
fortify the rule of the bourgeoisie over the proletariat.

Marx's philosophy is matured philosophical materialism, which has provided humanity, and especially
the working class, with powerful instruments of
knowledge.

II

Having recognized that the economic system is the
foundation on which the political superstructure is
erected, Marx devoted most attention to the study of
this economic system. Marx's principal work, *Capital*,
is devoted to a study of the economic system of modern, i.e., capitalist, society.

Classical political economy, before Marx, evolved
in England, the most developed of the capitalist countries. Adam Smith and David Ricardo, by their investigations of the economic system, laid the foundations
of the *labor theory of value*. Marx continued their work.
He rigidly proved and consistently developed this
theory. He showed that the value of every commodity
is determined by the quantity of socially necessary
labor time spent on its production.

Where the bourgeois economists saw a relation of
things (the exchange of one commodity for another),
Marx revealed a *relation of men*. The exchange of
commodities expresses the tie by which individual
producers are bound through the market. *Money* signifies that this tie is becoming closer and closer,
inseparably binding the entire economic life of the
individual producers into one whole. *Capital* signifies
a further development of this tie: man's labor power
becomes a commodity. The wage-worker sells labor
power to the owner of the land, factories and instruments of labor. The worker uses one part of the labor
day to cover the expense of maintaining himself and

his family (wages), while the other part of the day the worker toils without remuneration, creating *surplus value* for the capitalist, the source of profit, the source of the wealth of the capitalist class.

The doctrine of surplus value is the cornerstone of Marx's economic theory.

Capital, created by the labor of the worker, presses on the worker by ruining the small masters and creating an army of unemployed. In industry, the victory of large-scale production is at once apparent, but we observe the same phenomenon in agriculture as well: the superiority of large-scale capitalist agriculture increases, the application of machinery grows, peasant economy falls into the noose of money-capital, it declines and sinks into ruin, burdened by its backward technique. In agriculture, the decline of small-scale production assumes different forms, but the decline itself is an indisputable fact.

By destroying small-scale production, capital leads to an increase in productivity of labor and to the creation of a monopoly position for the associations of big capitalists. Production itself becomes more and more social—hundreds of thousands and millions of workers become bound together in a systematic economic organism—but the product of the collective labor is appropriated by a handful of capitalists. The anarchy of production grows, as do crises, the furious chase after markets and the insecurity of existence of the mass of the population.

While increasing the dependence of the workers on capital, the capitalist system creates the great power of united labor.

Marx traced the development of capitalism from the first germs of commodity economy, from simple exchange, to its highest forms, to large-scale production.

And the experience of all capitalist countries, old

and new, is clearly demonstrating the truth of this Marxian doctrine to increasing numbers of workers every year.

Capitalism has triumphed all over the world, but this triumph is only the prelude to the triumph of labor over capital.

III

When feudalism was overthrown, and *"free"* capitalist society appeared on God's earth, it at once became apparent that this freedom meant a new system of oppression and exploitation of the toilers. Various socialist doctrines immediately began to rise as a reflection of and protest against this oppression. But early socialism was *utopian* socialism. It criticized capitalist society, it condemned and damned it, it dreamed of its destruction, it indulged in fancies of a better order and endeavored to convince the rich of the immorality of exploitation.

However, utopian socialism could not point the real way out. It could not explain the essence of wage-slavery under capitalism, nor discover the laws of its development, nor point to the *social force* which is capable of becoming the creator of a new society.

Meanwhile, the stormy revolutions which everywhere in Europe, and especially in France, accompanied the fall of feudalism, of serfdom, more and more clearly revealed the *struggle of classes* as the basis and the motive force of the whole development.

Not a single victory of political freedom over the feudal class was won except against desperate resistance. Not a single capitalist country evolved on a more or less free and democratic basis except by a life and death struggle between the various classes of capitalist society.

The genius of Marx consists in the fact that he was

able before anybody else to draw from this and apply consistently the deduction that world history teaches. This deduction is the doctrine of the *class struggle*.

People always were and always will be the stupid victims of deceit and self-deceit in politics until they learn to discover the *interests* of some class behind all moral, religious, political and social phrases, declarations and promises. The supporters of reforms and improvements will always be fooled by the defenders of the old order until they realize that every old institution, however barbarous and rotten it may appear to be, is maintained by the forces of some ruling classes. And there is *only one* way of smashing the resistance of these classes, and that is to find, in the very society which surrounds us, and to enlighten and organize for the struggle, the forces which can—and, owing to their social position, *must*—constitute a power capable of sweeping away the old and creating the new.

Marx's philosophical materialism has alone shown the proletariat the way out of the spiritual slavery in which all oppressed classes have hitherto languished. Marx's economic theory has alone explained the true position of the proletariat in the general system of capitalism.

Independent organizations of the proletariat are multiplying all over the world, from America to Japan and from Sweden to South Africa. The proletariat is becoming enlightened and educated by waging its class struggle; it is ridding itself of the prejudices of bourgeois society; it is rallying its ranks ever more closely and is learning to gauge the measure of its successes; it is steeling its forces and is growing irresistibly.

March 1913

7. THE HISTORICAL DESTINY OF THE DOCTRINE OF KARL MARX

THE main thing in the doctrine of Marx is that it brings out the historic role of the proletariat as the builder of a socialist society. Has the progress of world events confirmed this doctrine since it was expounded by Marx?

Marx first advanced it in 1844. The *Communist Manifesto* of Marx and Engels, published in 1848, already gives a complete and systematic exposition of this doctrine, which has remained the best exposition to this day. Subsequent world history clearly falls into three main periods: (1) from the Revolution of 1848 to the Paris Commune (1871); (2) from the Paris Commune to the Russian Revolution (1905); (3) since the Russian Revolution.

Let us see what has been the destiny of Marx's doctrine in each of these periods.

I

At the beginning of the first period Marx's doctrine by no means dominated. It was only one of the extremely numerous factions or trends of socialism. The forms of socialism which did dominate were in the main akin to our *Narodism*[1]: noncomprehension of the materialist basis of historical movement, inability to assign the role and significance of each class in capitalist society, concealment of the bourgeois essence of democratic reforms under diverse, pseudo-socialistic phrases about "the people," "justice," "right," etc.

· The Revolution of 1848 struck a fatal blow at all these vociferous, motley and ostentatious forms of *pre*-Marxian socialism. In all countries the revolution revealed the various classes of society *in action*. The shooting down of the workers by the republican bourgeoisie in the June Days of 1848 in Paris finally established that the proletariat *alone* was socialist by nature. The craven liberals groveled before reaction. The peasantry were content with the abolition of the relics of feudalism and joined the supporters of order, only wavering at times between *the democratic workers and the bourgeois liberals*. All doctrines of *non*-class socialism and *non*-class politics proved to be sheer nonsense.

The Paris Commune (1871) completed this development of bourgeois reforms; the republic, i.e., the form of state organization in which class relations appear in their most unconcealed form, had only the heroism of the proletariat to thank for its consolidation.

In all the other European countries a more entangled and less finished development also led to a definitely shaped bourgeois society. Towards the end of the first period (1848–71)—a period of storms and revolutions—pre-Marxian socialism *died away*. Independent *proletarian* parties were born: the First International (1864–72) and the German Social-Democratic Party.

II

The second period (1872–1904) was distinguished from the first by its "peaceful" character, by the absence of revolutions. The West had finished with bourgeois revolutions. The East had not yet arrived at the stage of bourgeois revolutions.

The West entered a phase of "peaceful" preparation for the future era of change. Socialist parties, basically proletarian, were formed everywhere and learned to make use of bourgeois parliamentarism and to create their own daily press, their educational institutions, their trade unions and their cooperative societies. The Marxian doctrine gained a complete victory and *spread*. The process of selection and accumulation of the forces of the proletariat and of the preparation of the proletariat for the impending battles progressed slowly but steadily.

The dialectics of history were such that the theoretical victory of Marxism obliged its enemies to *disguise themselves* as Marxists. Liberalism, rotten to the core, attempted a revival in the form of Socialist *opportunism*. The opportunists interpreted the period of preparation of forces for the great battles as a renunciation of these battles. The improvement of the position of the slaves for the struggle against wage slavery they represented as the necessity for the slaves to sell their right to liberty for a mess of pottage. They pusillanimously preached "social peace" (i.e., peace with the slave owners), the renunciation of the class struggle, and so forth. They had many adherents among Socialist members of Parliament, various officials of the labor movement, and the "sympathetic" intellectuals.

III

Scarcely had the opportunists congratulated themselves on "social peace" and the needlessness of storms under "democracy" when a new source of great world storms opened up in Asia. The Russian revolution was followed by the Turkish, the Persian and the Chinese revolutions. It is in this era of storms and their "repercussion" on Europe that we are now living. Whatever may be the fate of the great Chinese Republic, against which the various "civilized" hyenas are now baring their teeth, no power on earth can restore the old serfdom in Asia, or wipe out the heroic democracy of the masses of the people in the Asian and semi-Asian countries.

Certain people, who were inattentive to the conditions of preparation and development of the mass struggle, were driven to despair and to anarchism by the prolonged postponements of the decisive struggle against capitalism in Europe. We can now see how short-sighted and pusillanimous this anarchist despair is.

The fact that Asia, with its population of eight hundred million, has been drawn into the struggle for these same European ideals should inspire us with courage and not despair.

The Asian revolutions have revealed the same spinelessness and baseness of liberalism, the same exceptional importance of the independence of the democratic masses, and the same sharp line of division between the proletariat and the bourgeoisie of all kinds. After the experience both of Europe and Asia, whoever now speaks of *non*-class politics and of *non*-class Socialism simply deserves to be put in a cage and exhibited alongside of the Australian kangaroo.

After Asia, Europe has also begun to stir, although not in the Asian way. The "peaceful" period of 1872–1904 has passed completely, never to return. The high cost of living and the oppression of the trusts is leading to an unprecedented accentuation of the economic struggle, which has roused even the British workers, who have been most corrupted by liberalism. Before our eyes a political crisis is brewing even in that extreme "diehard," bourgeois-Junker country, Germany. Feverish armaments and the policy of imperialism are turning modern Europe into a "social peace" which is more like a barrel of gunpowder than anything else. And at the same time the decay of *all* the bourgeois parties and the maturing of the proletariat are progressing steadily.

Each of the three great periods of world history since the appearance of Marxism has brought Marxism new confirmation and new triumphs. But a still greater triumph awaits Marxism as the doctrine of the proletariat in the period of history that is now opening.

March 1913

8. KARL MARX

Karl Marx was born May 5, 1818, in the city of Trier (Rhenish Prussia). His father was a lawyer, a Jew who in 1824 adopted Protestantism. The family was well-to-do, cultured, but not revolutionary. After graduating from the *gymnasium* in Trier, Marx entered the university, first at Bonn and later at Berlin, where he studied jurisprudence and, chiefly, history and philosophy. He concluded his course in 1841, submitting his doctoral dissertation on the philosophy of Epicurus. In his views Marx at that time was still a Hegelian idealist. In Berlin he belonged to the circle of "Left Hegelians" (Bruno Bauer and others) who sought to draw atheistic and revolutionary conclusions from Hegel's philosophy.

After graduating from the university, Marx moved to Bonn, expecting to become a professor. But the reactionary policy of the government—which in 1832 deprived Ludwig Feuerbach of his chair and in 1836 refused to allow him to return to the university, and in 1841 forbade the young professor, Bruno Bauer, to lecture at Bonn—forced Marx to abandon the idea of pursuing an academic career. At that time the views of the Left Hegelians were developing very rapidly in Germany. Ludwig Feuerbach, particularly after 1836, began to criticize theology and to turn to materialism, which in 1841 gained the upper hand in his philosophy (*Das Wesen des Christentums* [*The Essence of Christianity*]); in 1843 his *Grundsätze der Philosophe der Zukunft* (*Principles of the Philosoply of the Future*) appeared. "One must himself have experienced the liberating effect" of these books, Engels subsequently wrote of these works of Feuerbach. "We [i.e., the Left Hegelians, including Marx] all became at once Feuerbachians."[1] At that time some Rhenish radical bourgeois who had certain points in common with the Left Hegelians founded an opposition paper in Cologne, the *Rheinische Zeitung* (*Rhenish Gazette*); the first number appeared on January 1, 1842. Marx and Bruno Bauer were invited to be the chief contributors, and in October 1842 Marx became chief editor and moved from Bonn to Cologne. The revolutionary-democratic trend of the paper became more and more pronounced under Marx's editorship, and the government first subjected the paper to double and triple censorship and then on January 1, 1843, decided to suppress it altogether. Marx had to resign the editorship before that date, but his resignation did not save the paper, which was closed down in March 1843. Of the more important articles contributed by Marx to the *Rheinische Zeitung*, Engels notes, in addition to those indicated below (see "Bibliography"),[2] an article on the condition of the peasant wine-growers of the Moselle Valley. His journalistic activities convinced Marx that he was not sufficiently acquainted with political economy, and he zealously set out to study it.

In 1843, in Kreuznach, Marx married Jenny von Westphalen, a childhood friend to whom he had been engaged while still a student. His wife came from a reactionary family of the Prussian nobility. Her elder brother was Prussian Minister of the Interior at a most reactionary period, 1850–58. In the autumn of 1843 Marx went to Paris in order, together with Arnold Ruge (born 1802, died 1880; a Left Hegelian; in 1825–30, in prison; after 1848, a political exile; after 1866–70, a Bismarckian), to publish a radical magazine abroad. Only one issue of this magazine, *Deutsch-Französische Jahrbücher* (*German-French Annals*) appeared. It was discontinued owing to the difficulty of secret distribution in Germany and to disagreements with Ruge. In his articles in this magazine Marx already appears as a revolutionary; he advocates the "merciless criticism of everything existing," and in particular the "criticism of arms,"[3] and appeals to the *masses* and to the *proletariat*.

In September 1844 Frederick Engels came to Paris for a few days, and from that time forth became Marx's closest friend. They both took a most active part in the then seething life of the revolutionary groups in Paris (of particular importance was Proudhon's doctrine, which Marx thoroughly demolished in his *Poverty of Philosophy*, 1847), and vigorously combating the various doctrines of petty-bourgeois Socialism, worked out the theory and tactics of revolutionary *proletarian Socialism*, or Communism (Marxism). See Marx's works of this period, 1844–48, in the "Bibliography."[4] In 1845, on the insistent demand of the Prussian government, Marx was banished from Paris as a dangerous revolutionary. He moved to Brussels. In the spring of 1847 Marx and Engels joined a secret propaganda society called the Communist League, took a prominent part in the Second Congress of the League (London, November 1847), and at its request drew up the famous *Communist Manifesto*, which appeared in February 1848. With the clarity and brilliance of genius, this work outlines the new world conception, consistent materialism, which also embraces the realm of social life, dialectics, the most comprehensive and profound doctrine of development, the theory of the class struggle and of the historic revolutionary role of the proletariat—the creator of the new, communist society.

When the Revolution of February 1848 broke out, Marx was banished from Belgium. He returned to Paris, whence, after the March Revolution, he went to Germany, again to Cologne. There the *Neue Rheinische Zeitung* (*New Rhenish Gazette*) appeared from June 1, 1848, to May 19, 1849; Marx was the chief editor. The new theory was brilliantly corroborated by the course of the revolutionary events of 1848–49, as it has been since corroborated by all proletarian and democratic movements of all countries in the world. The victorious counter-revolution first instigated court proceedings against Marx (he was acquitted on February 9, 1849) and then banished him from Germany (May 16, 1849). Marx first went to Paris, was again banished after the demonstration of June 13, 1849, and then went to London, where he lived to the day of his death.

His life as a political exile was a very hard one, as the correspondence between Marx and Engels (published in 1913)* clearly reveals. Marx and his family suffered dire poverty. Were it not for Engels' constant and self-sacrificing support, Marx would not only have been unable to finish *Capital* but would have inevitably perished from want. Moreover, the prevailing doctrines and trends of petty-bourgeois Socialism, and of non-proletarian Socialism in general, forced Marx to

---

*Hereafter referred to as the *Briefwechsel* (*Correspondence*).—Ed.*

carry on a continuous and merciless fight and some-times to repel the most savage and monstrous personal attacks (*Herr Vogt*).[5] Holding aloof from the circles of political exiles, Marx developed his materialist theory in a number of historic works[6], devoting his efforts chiefly to the study of political economy. Marx revolutionized this this science (see below, "Marx's Teachings") in his *Contribution to the Critique of Political Economy* (1859) and *Capital* (Vol. I, 1867).

The period of revival of the democratic movements at the end of the 'fifties and the 'sixties recalled Marx to practical activity. In 1864 (September 28) the International Working Men's Association—the famous First International—was founded in London. Marx was the heart and soul of this organization; he was the author of its first Address and of a host of resolutions, declarations and manifestoes.[7] By uniting the labor movement of various countries, by striving to direct into the channel of joint activity the various forms of non-proletarian, pre-Marxian Socialism (Mazzini, Proudhon, Bakunin, liberal trade unionism in England, Lassallean vacillations to the Right in Germany, etc.), and by combating the theories of all these sects and schools, Marx hammered out a uniform tactic for the proletarian struggle of the working class in the various countries. After the fall of the Paris Commune (1871)—of which Marx gave such a profound, clear-cut, brilliant, *effective* and revolutionary analysis (*The Civil War in France*, 1871), and after the International was split by the Bakuninists, the existence of that organization in Europe became impossible. After the Hague Congress of the International (1872) Marx had the General Council of the International transferred to New York. The First International had accomplished its historical role, and it made way for a period of immeasurably larger growth of the labor movement in all the countries of the world, a period, in fact, when the movement grew in *breadth* and when *mass* Socialist labor parties in individual national states were created.

His strenuous work in the International and his still more strenuous theoretical occupations completely undermined Marx's health. He continued his work on the reshaping of political economy and the completion of *Capital,* for which he collected a mass of new material and studied a number of languages (Russian, for instance); but ill-health prevented him from finishing *Capital.*[8]

On December 2, 1881, his wife died. On March 14, 1883, Marx peacefully passed away in his armchair. He lies buried with his wife and Helene Demuth, their devoted servant who was almost a member of the family, in the Highgate Cemetery, London.

MARX'S TEACHINGS

Marxism is the system of the views and teachings of Marx. Marx was the genius who continued and completed the three main ideological currents of the nineteenth century, belonging to the three most advanced countries of mankind: classical German philosophy, classical English political economy, and French Socialism together with French revolutionary doctrines in general. The remarkable consistency and integrity of Marx's views, acknowledged even by his opponents, views which in their totality constitute modern materialism and modern scientific Socialism, as the theory and program of the labor movement in all the civilized countries of the world, oblige us to present a brief outline of his world conception in general before proceeding to the exposition of the principal content of Marxism, namely, Marx's economic doctrine.

Philosophical Materialism

From 1844–45, when his views took shape, Marx was a materialist, in particular a follower of L. Feuerbach, whose weak sides he even later considered to consist exclusively in the fact that his materialism was not consistent and comprehensive enough. Marx regarded the historic and "epoch-making" importance of Feuerbach to be that he had resolutely broken away from Hegelian idealism and had proclaimed materialism, which already in the eighteenth century, especially in France, "had been a struggle not only against the existing political institutions and against . . . religion and theology, but also . . . against all metaphysics" (in the sense of "intoxicated speculation" as distinct from "sober philosophy"). (*The Holy Family* in the *Literarischer Nachlass*).

"To Hegel . . . " wrote Marx, "the process of thinking, which, under the name of 'the Idea,' he even transforms into an independent subject, is the demiurgos [the creator, the maker] of the real world. . . . With me, on the contrary, the idea is nothing else than the material world reflected by the human mind, and translated into forms of thought."[9]

In full conformity with this materialist philosophy of Marx's, and expounding it, Frederick Engels wrote in *Anti-Dühring* (which Marx read in manuscript):

"The unity of the world does not consist in its being. . . . The real unity of the world consists in its materiality, and this is proved . . . by a long and protracted development of philosophy and natural science. . . . *Motion is the mode of existence of matter.* Never anywhere has there been matter without motion, nor can there be. . . . But if the . . . question is raised: what then are thought and consciousness, and whence they come, it becomes apparent that they are products of the human brain and that man himself is a product of nature, which has been developed in and along with its environment; whence it is self-evident that the products of the human brain, being in the last analysis also products of nature, do not contradict the rest of nature but are in correspondence with it.

"Hegel was an idealist, that is to say, the thoughts within his mind were to him not the more or less abstract images [*Abbilder*, reflections; Engels sometimes speaks of "imprints"] of real things and processes, but, on the contrary, things and their development were to him only the images made real of the 'Idea' existing somewhere or other already before the world existed."[10]

In his *Ludwig Feuerbach*—in which he expounds his and Marx's views on Feuerbach's philosophy, and which he sent to the press after re-reading an old manuscript written by Marx and himself in 1844–45 on Hegel, Feuerbach and the materialist conception of history—Frederick Engels writes:

"The great basic question of all philosophy, especially of modern philosophy, is that concerning the relation of thinking and being . . . spirit to nature . . . which is primary, spirit or nature. . . . The answers which the philosophers gave to this question split them into two great camps. Those who asserted the primacy of spirit to nature and, therefore, in the last instance, assumed world creation in some form or other . . . comprised the camp of idealism. The others, who regarded nature as primary, belong to the various schools of materialism."[11]

Any other use of the concepts of (philosophical) idealism and materialism leads only to confusion. Marx decidedly rejected not only idealism, always connected in one way or another with religion, but also the views, especially widespread in our day, of Hume and Kant, agnosticism, criticism, positivism in their various forms, regarding such a philosophy as a "reactionary" concession to idealism and at best a "shamefaced way of surreptitiously accepting materialism, while denying it before the world.[12] On this question, see, in addition to the above-mentioned works of Engels and Marx, a letter of Marx to Engels dated December 12, 1866, in which Marx, referring to an utterance of the well-known naturalist, Thomas Huxley, that was "more materialistic" than usual, and to his recognition that "as long as we actually observe and think, we cannot possibly get away from materialism," at the same time reproaches him for leaving a "loop-hole" for agnosticism and Humeism.

It is espcially important to note Marx's view on the relation between freedom and necessity: "Freedom is the appreciation of necessity. 'Necessity is *blind only in so far as it is not understood*'" (Engels, *Anti-Dühring*).[13] This means the recognition of objective law in nature and of the dialectical transformation of necessity into freedom (in the same manner as the transformation of the unknown, but knowable, "thing-in-itself" into the "thing-for-us," of the "essence of things" into "phenomena"). Marx and Engels considered the fundamental limitations of the "old" materialism, including the materialism of Feuerbach (and still more of the "vulgar" materialism of Büchner, Vogt and Moleschott), to be: (1) that this materialism was "predominantly mechanical," failing to take account of the latest developments of chemistry and biology (in our day it would be necessary to add: and of the electrical theory of matter); (2) that the old materialism was non-historical, non-dialectical (metaphysical, in the sense of anti-dialectical), and did not arhere consistently and comprehensively to the standpoint of development; (3) that it regarded the "human essence" abstractly and not as the *"ensemble"* of all concretely defined historical "social relations," and therefore only "interpreted" the world, whereas the point is to "change" it; that is to say, it did not understand the importance of "revolutionary, practical-critical, activity."

Dialectics

Hegelian dialectics, as the most comprehensive, the most rich in content, and the most profound doctrine of development, was regarded by Marx and Engels as the greatest achievement of classical German philosophy. They considered every other formulation of the principle of development, of evolution, one-sided and poor in content, and distorting and mutilating the real course of development (often proceeding by leaps, catastrophes and revolutions) in nature and in society.

"Marx and I were pretty well the only people to rescue conscious dialectics [from the destruction of idealism, including Hegelianism] and apply it in the materialist conception of nature. . . . Nature is the test of dialectics, and it must be said for modern natural science that it has furnished extremely rich [this was written before the discovery of radium, electrons, the transmutation of elements, etc.!] and daily increasing materials for this test, and has thus proved that in the last analysis nature's process is dialectical and not metaphysical."[14]

"The great basic thought," Engels writes, "that the world is not to be comprehended as a complex of ready-made *things*, but as a complex of *processes*, in which the things apparently stable, no less than their mind-images in our heads, the concepts, go through an uninterrupted change of coming into being and passing away . . . this great fundamental thought has, especially since the time of Hegel, so thoroughly permeated ordinary consciousness that in this generality it is scarcely ever contradicted. But to acknowledge this fundamental thought in words and to apply it in reality in detail to each domain of investigation are two different things.

"For it [dialectical philosophy] nothing is final, absolute, sacred. It reveals the transitory character of everything and in everything; nothing can endure before it except the uninterrupted process of becoming and of passing away, of endless ascendency from the lower to the higher. And dialectical philosophy itself is nothing more than the mere reflection of this process in the thinking brain." Thus, according to Marx, dialectics is "the science of the general laws of motion—both of the external world and of human thought."[15]

This revolutionary side of Hegel's philosophy was adopted and developed by Marx. Dialectical materialism "no longer needs any philosophy standing above the other sciences." Of former philosophy there remains "the science of thought and its laws—formal logic and dialectics."[16] And dialectics, as understood by Marx, and in conformity with Hegel, includes what is now called the theory of knowledge, or epistemology, which, too, must regard its subject matter historically, studying and generalizing the origin and development of knowledge, the transition from *non-knowledge* to knowledge.

Nowadays, the idea of development, of evolution, has penetrated the social consciousness almost in its entirety, but by different ways, not by way of the Hegelian philosophy. But as formulated by Marx and Engels on the basis of Hegel, this idea is far more comprehensive, far richer in content than the current idea of evolution. A development that seemingly repeats the stages already passed, but repeats them otherwise, on a higher basis ("negation of negation"), a development, so to speak, in spirals, not in a straight line;—a development by leaps, catastrophes, revolutions;—"breaks in continuity";—the transformation of quantity into quality;—the inner impulses to development, imparted by the contradiction and conflict of the various forces and tendencies acting on a given body, or within a given phenomenon, or within a given society;—the interdependence and the closest, indissoluble connection of *all* sides of every phenomenon (while history constantly discloses ever new sides), a connection that provides a uniform, law-governed, universal process of motion—such are some of the features of dialectics as a richer (than the ordinary) doctrine of development. (See Marx's letter to Engels of January 8, 1868, in which he ridicules Stein's "wooden trichotomies," which it would be absurd to confuse with materialist dialectics.)

The Materialist Conception of History

Having realized the inconsistency, incompleteness, and one-sidedness of the old materialism, Marx became convinced of the necessity of "bringing the science of society . . . into harmony with the materialist foundation, and of reconstructing it thereupon."[17] Since materialism in general explains consciousness as the outcome of being, and not conversely, materialism as applied to the social life of mankind had to explain *social* consciousness as the outcome of *social* being.

"Technology," writes Marx, "discloses man's mode of dealing with nature, the process of production by which he sustains his life, and thereby also lays bare the mode of formation of his social relations, and of the mental conceptions that flow from them."[18]

In the preface to his *Contribution to the Critique of Political Economy*, Marx gives an integral formulation of the fundamental principles of materialism as extended to human society and its history, in the following words:

"In the social production which men carry on they enter into definite relations that are indispensable and independent of their will; these relations of production correspond to a definite stage of development of their material forces of production. The sum total of these relations of production constitutes the economic structure of society—the real foundation, on which rises a legal and political superstructure and to which correspond definite forms of social consciousness. The mode of production in material life determines the social, political and intellectual life processes in general. It is not the consciousness of men that determines their being, but, on the contrary, their social being that determines their consciousness. At a certain stage of their development, the material forces of production in society come in conflict with the existing relations of production, or—what is but a legal expression for the same thing—with the property relations within which they have been at work before. From forms of development of the forces of production these relations turn into their fetters. Then begins an epoch of social revolution. With the change of the economic foundation the entire immense superstructure is more or less rapidly transformed. In considering such transformations a distinction should always be made between the material transformation of the economic conditions of production, which can be determined with the precision of natural science, and the legal, political, religious, esthetic or philosophic—in short, ideological forms in which men become conscious of this conflict and fight it out. Just as our opinion of an individual is not based on what he thinks of himself, so can we not judge of such a period of transformation by its own consciousness; on the contrary, this consciousnes must be explained rather from the contradictions of material life, from the existing conflict between the social forces of production and the relations of production. . . . In broad outlines we can designate the Asiatic, the ancient, the feudal, and the modern bourgeois modes of production as so may epochs in the progress of the economic formation of society."[19] (*See* Marx's brief formulation in a letter to Engels dated July 7, 1866: "Our theory that the organization of labor is determined by the means of production.")

The discovery of the materialist conception of history, or rather, the consistent extension of materialism to the domain of social phenomena, removed two of the chief defects of earlier historical theories. In the first place, they at best examined only the ideological motïves of the historical activity of human beings, without investigating what produced these motives, without grasping the objective laws governing the development of the system of social relations, and without discerning the roots of these relations in the degree of development of material production. In the second place, the earlier theories did not cover the activities of the *masses* of the population, whereas historical materialism made it possible for the first time to study with the accuracy of the natural sciences the social conditions of the life of the masses and the changes in these conditions. Pre-Marxian "sociology" and historiography *at best* provided an accumulation of raw facts, collected at random, and a depiction of certain sides of the historical process. By examining the *ensemble* of all the opposing tendencies, by reducing them to precisely definable conditions of life and production of the various *classes* of society, by discarding subjectivism and arbitrariness in the choice of various "leading" ideas or in their interpretation, and by disclosing that all ideas and all the various tendencies, without exception, have their *roots* in the condition of the material forces of production, Marxism pointed the way to an all-embracing and comprehensive study of the process of rise, development, and decline of social-economic formations. People make their own history. But what determines the motives of people, of the mass of people; that is: what gives rise to the clash of conflicting ideas and strivings; what is the ensemble of all these clashes of the whole mass of human societies; what are the objective conditions of production of material life that form the basis of all historical activity of man; what is the law of development of these conditions—to all this Marx drew attention and pointed out the way to a scientific study of history as a unifrom and law-governed process in all its immense variety and contradictions.

The Class Struggle

That in any given society the strivings of some of its members conflict with the strivings of others, that social life is full of contradictions, that history discloses a struggle between nations and societies as well as within nations and societies, and, in addition, an alternation of periods of revolution and reaction, peace and war, stagnation and rapid progress or decline—are facts that are generally known. Marxism provided the clue which enables us to discover the laws governing this seeming labyrinth and chaos, namely, the theory of the class struggle. Only a study of the ensemble of strivings of all the members of a given society or group of societies can lead to a scientific definition of the result of these strivings. And the source of the conflict of strivings lies in the difference in the position and mode of life of the *classes* into which each society is divided.

"The history of all hitherto existing society is the history of class struggles," wrote Marx in the *Communist Manifesto* (except the history of the primitive community, Engels added).

"Freeman and slave, patrician and plebeian, lord and serf, guild-master and journeyman, in a word, oppressor and oppressed, stood in constant opposition to one another, carried on an uninterrupted, now hidden, now open fight, a fight that each time ended, either in a revolutionary reconstitution of society at large, or in the common ruin of the contending classes. . . .

"The modern bourgeois society that has sprouted from the ruins of feudal society has not done away with class antagonisms. It has but established new classes, new conditions of oppression, new forms of struggle in place of the old ones.

"Our epoch, the epoch of the bourgeoisie, possesses, however, this distinctive feature: it has simplified the class antagonisms. Society as a whole is more and more splitting up into two great hostile camps, into two great classes directly facing each other—bourgeoisie and proletariat."[20]

Ever since the Great French Revolution, European history has very clearly revealed in a number of countries this real undersurface of events, the struggle of classes. And the Restoration period in France already produced a number of historians (Thierry, Guizot, Mignet, Thiers) who, generalizing from events, were forced to recognize that the class struggle was the key to all French history. And the modern era—the era of the complete victory of the bourgeoisie, representative institutions, wide (if not universal) suffrage, a cheap, popular daily press, etc., the era of powerful and ever-expanding unions of workers and unions of employers, etc.—has revealed even more manifestly (though sometimes in a very one-sided, "peaceful," "constitutional" form) that the class struggle is the mainspring of events. The following passage from Marx's *Communist Manifesto* will show us what Marx required of social science in respect to an objective analysis of the position of each class in modern society in connection with an analysis of the conditions of development of each class:

"Of all the classes that stand face to face with the bourgeoisie today, the proletariat alone is a really revolutionary class. The other classes decay and finally disappear in the face of modern industry; the proletariat is its special and essential product.

"The lower middle class, the small manufacturer, the shopkeeper, the artisan, the peasant, all these fight against the bourgeoisie to save from extinction their existence as fractions of the lower middle class. They are therefore not revolutionary, but conservative. Nay more, they are reactionary, for they try to roll back the wheel of history. If by chance they are revolutionary, they are only so in view of their impending transfer into the proletariat; they thus defend not their present, but their future interests; they desert their own standpoint to adopt that of the proletariat."[21]

In a number of historic works (see "Bibliography"), Marx has given us brilliant and profound examples of materialist historiography, of an analysis of the position of *each* individual class, and sometimes of various groups or strata within a class, showing plainly why and how "every class struggle is a political struggle." The above-quoted passage is an illustration of what a complex network of social relations and *transitional* stages between one class and another, from the past to the future, Marx analyzes in order to determine the resultant of historical development.

The most profound, comprehensive and detailed confirmation and application of Marx's theory is his economic doctrine.

Marx's Economic Doctrine

"It is the ultimate aim of this work to lay bare the economic law of motion of modern society" (that is to say, capitalist, bourgeois society), says Marx in the preface to *Capital*. The investigation of the relations of production in a given, historically defined society, in their genesis, development, and decline—such is the content of Marx's economic doctrine. In capitalist society it is the production of *commodities* that dominates, and Marx's analysis therefore begins with an analysis of the commodity.

Value

A commodity is, in the first place, a thing that satisfies a human want; in the second place, it is a thing that can be exchanged for another thing. The utility of a thing makes it a *use-value*. Exchange-value (or simply, value) presents itself first of all as a relation, as the proportion in which a certain number of use-values of one sort are exchanged for a certain number of use-values of another sort. Daily experience shows us that millions upon millions of such exchanges are constantly equating one with another every kind of use-value, even the most diverse and incomparable. Now, what is there in common between these various things, things constantly equated one with another in a definite system of social relations? What is common to them is that they are *products of labor*. In exchanging products people equate to one another the most diverse kinds of labor. The production of commodities is a system of social relations in which the single producers create diverse products (the social division of labor), and in which all these products are equated to one another in exchange. Consequently, what is common to all commodities is not the concrete labor of a definite branch of production, not labor of one particular kind, but *abstract* human labor—human labor in general. All the labor power of a given society, as represented in the sum total of values of all commodities, is one and the same human labor power; millions and millions of acts of exchange prove this. And, consequently, each particular commodity represents only a certain share of the *socially necessary* labor time. The magnitude of value is determined by the amount of socially necessary labor, or by the labor time that is socially necessary for the production of the given commodity, of the given use-value.

" . . . Whenever, by an exchange, we equate as values our different products, by that very act, we also equate, as human labor, the different kinds of labor expended upon them. We are not aware of this, nevertheless we do it." As one of the earlier economists said, value is a relation between two persons; only he ought to have added: a relation between persons expressed as a relation between things. We can understand what value is only when we consider it from the standpoint of the system of social relations of production of one particular historical formation of society; relations, moreover, which manifest themselves in the mass phenomenon of exchange, a phenomenon which repeats itself millions upon millions of times. "As values, all commodities are only definite masses of congealed labor time."[22]

Having made a detailed analysis of the twofold character of the labor incorporated in commodities, Marx goes on to analyze the *forms of value* and *money*. Marx's main task here is to study the *origin* of the money form of value, to study the *historical process* of development of exchange, from isolated and casual acts of exchange ("elementary or accidental form of value," in which a given quantity of one commodity is exchanged for a given quantity of another) to the universal form of value, in which a number of different commodities are exchanged for one and the same particular commodity, and to the money form of value, when gold becomes this particular commodity, the universal equivalent. Being the highest product of the development of exchange and commodity production, money masks and conceals the social character of all individual labor, the social tie between the individual producers who are united by the market. Marx analyzes in great detail the various functions of money; and it is essential to note here in particular (as generally in the opening chapters of *Capital*), that the abstract and seemingly at times purely deductive mode of exposition in reality reproduces a gigantic collection of factual material on the history of the development of exchange and commodity production.

" . . . If we consider money, its existence implies a definite stage in the exchange of commodities. The particular functions of money which it performs, either as the mere equivalent of commodities, or as means of circulation, or means of payment, as hoard or as universal money, point, according to the extent and relative preponderance of the one function or the other, to very different stages in the process of social production"[23].

Surplus Value

At a certain stage in the development of commodity production money becomes transformed into capital. The formula of commodity circulation was C—M—C (commodity—money—commodity), i.e., the sale of one commodity for the purpose of buying another. The general formula of capital, on the contrary, is M—C—M (money—commodity—money), i.e., purchase for the purpose of selling (at a profit). The increase over the original value of money put into circulation Marx calls surplus value. The fact of this "growth" of money in capitalist circulation is well known. It is this "growth" which transforms money into *capital,* as a special, historically defined, social relation of production. Surplus value cannot arise out of commodity circulation, for the latter knows only the exchange of equivalents; it cannot arise out of an addition to price, for the mutual losses and gains of buyers and sellers would equalize one another, whereas what we have here is not an individual phenomenon but a mass, average, social phenomenon. In order to derive surplus value, the owner of money "must . . . find . . . in the market a commodity whose use-value possesses the peculiar property of being a source of value"[24] —a commodity whose process of consumption is at the same time a process of creation of value. And such a commodity exists. It is human labor power. Its consumption is labor, and labor creates value. The owner of money buys labor power at its value, which, like the value of every other commodity, is determined by the socially necessary labor time requisite for its production (i.e., the cost of maintaining the worker and his family).

Having bought labor power, the owner of money is entitled to use it, that is, to set it to work for the whole day—twelve hours, let us suppose. Yet, in the course of six hours ("necessary" labor time) the laborer produces product sufficient to cover the cost of his own maintenance; and in the course of the next six hours ("surplus value" labor time), he produces "surplus" product, or surplus value, for which the capitalist does not pay. In capital, therefore, from the standpoint of the process of production, two parts must be distinguished: constant capital, expended on means of production (machinery, tools, raw materials, etc.), the value of which, without any change, is transferred (all at once or part by part) to the finished product; and variable capital, expended on labor power. The value of this latter capital is not invariable, but grows in the labor process, creating surplus value. Therefore, to express the degree of exploitation of labor power by capital, surplus value must be compared not with the whole capital but only with the variable capital. Thus in the example given, the rate of surplus value, as Marx calls this ratio, will be 6:6, i.e., 100 per cent.

The historical conditions necessary for the genesis of capital were, first, the accumulation of a certain sum of money in the hands of individuals and a relatively high level of development of commodity production in general, and, second, the existence of a laborer who is "free" in a double sense: free from all constraint or restriction on the sale of his labor power, and free from the land and of all means of production in general, a propertyless laborer, a "proletarian," who cannot subsist except by the sale of his labor power.

There are two principal methods by which surplus value can be increased: by lengthening the working day ("absolute surplus value"), and by shortening the necessary working day ("relative surplus value"). Analyzing the first method, Marx gives a most impressive picture of the struggle of the working class to shorten the working day and of governmental interference to lengthen the working day (from the fourteenth century to the seventeenth century) and to shorten the working day (factory legislation of the nineteenth century). Since the appearance of *Capital*, the history of the working-class movement in all civilized countries of the world has provided a wealth of new facts amplifying this picture.

Analyzing the production of relative surplus value,

Marx investigates the three main historical stages by which capitalism has increased the productivity of labor: (1) simple co-operation; (2) division of labor and manufacture; (3) machinery and large-scale industry. How profoundly Marx has here revealed the basic and typical features of capitalist development is incidentally shown by the fact that investigations of what is known as the "kustar" industry* of Russia furnish abundant material illustrating the first two of the mentioned stages. And the revolutionizing effect of large-scale machine industry, described by Marx in 1867, has been revealed in a number of "new" countries (Russia, Japan, etc.) in the course of the half-century that has since elapsed.

To continue. New and important in the highest degree is Marx's analysis of the *accumulation of capital,* i.e., the transformation of a part of surplus value into capital, its use, not for satisfying the personal needs or whims of the capitalist, but for new production. Marx revealed the mistake of all the earlier classical political economists (from Adam Smith on), who assumed that the entire surplus value which is transformed into capital goes to form variable capital. In actual fact, it is divided into *means of production* and variable capital. Of tremendous importance to the process of development of capitalism and its transformation into socialism is the more rapid growth of the constant capital share (of the total capital) as compared with the variable capital share.

The accumulation of capital, by accelerating the replacement of workers by machinery and creating wealth at one pole and poverty at the other, also gives rise to what is called the "reserve army of labor," to the

---

*Home industry.—*Ed.*

"relative surplus" of workers, or "capitalist overpopulation," which assumes the most diverse forms and enables capital to expand production at an extremely fast rate. This, in conjunction with credit facilities and the accumulation of capital in the means of production, incidentally furnishes the clue to the *crises* of overproduction that occur periodically in capitalist countries—at first at an average of every ten years, and later at more lengthy and less definite intervals. From the accumulation of capital under capitalism must be distinguished what is known as primitive accumulation: the forcible divorcement of the worker from the means of production, the driving of the peasants from the land, the stealing of the commons, the system of colonies and national debts, protective tariffs, and the like. "Primitive accumulation" creates the "free" proletarian at one pole, and the owner of money, the capitalist, at the other.

The *"historical tendency of capitalist accumulation"* is described by Marx in the following famous words:

"The expropriation of the immediate producers was accomplished with merciless vandalism, and under the stimulus of passions the most infamous, the most sordid, the pettiest, the most meanly odious. Self-earned private property [of the peasant and handicraftsman], that is based, so to say, on the fusing together of the isolated, independent laboring-individual with the conditions of his labor, is supplanted by capitalistic private property, which rests on exploitation of the nominally free labor of others. . . . That which is now to be expropriated is no longer the laborer working for himself, but the capitalist exploiting many laborers. This expropriation is accomplished by the action of the immanent laws of capitalistic production itself, by the centralization of capital. One capitalist always kills many. Hand in hand with this centralization, or this expropriation of many capitalists by few, develop, on an ever-extending scale, the cooperative form of the labor process, the conscious technical application of science, the methodical cultivation of the soil, the transformation of the instruments of labor into instruments of labor only usable in common, the economizing of all means of production by their use as the means of production of combined, socialized labor, the entanglement of all peoples in the net of the world market, and, with this, the international character of the capitalistic regime. Along with the constantly diminishing number of the magnates of capital, who usurp and monopolize all advantages of this process of transformation, grows the mass of misery, oppression, slavery, degradation, exploitation; but with this too grows the revolt of the working class, a class always increasing in numbers, and disciplined, united, organized by the very mechanism of the process of capitalist production itself. The monopoly of capital becomes a fetter upon the mode of production, which has sprung up and flourished along with and under it. Centralization of the means of production and socialization of labor at last reach a point where they become incompatible with their capitalist integument. This integument is burst asunder. The knell of capitalist private property sounds. The expropriators are expropriated."[25]

New and important in the highest degree, further, is the analysis Marx gives in the second volume of *Capital* of the reproduction of the aggregate social capital. Here, too, Marx deals not with an individual phenomenon but with a mass phenomenon; not with a fractional part of the economy of society but with this economy as a whole. Correcting the mistake of the classical economists mentioned above, Marx divides the entire social production into two big sections: (I) production of means of production, and (II) production of articles of consumption, and examines in detail, with arithmetical examples, the circulation of the aggregate social capital—both in the case of production in its former dimensions and in the case of accumulation.

The third volume of *Capital* solves the problem of the formation of the average rate of profit on the basis of the law of value. The immense advance in economic science made by Marx consists in the fact that he conducts his analysis from the standpoint of mass economic phenomena, of the social economy as a whole, and not from the standpoint of individual cases or of the external, superficial aspects of competition, to which vulgar political economy and the modern "theory of marginal utility" are frequently limited. Marx first analyzes the origin of surplus value, and then goes on to consider its division into profit, interest, and ground rent. Profit is the ratio between the surplus value and the total capital invested in an undertaking. Capital with a "high organic composition" (i.e., with a preponderance of constant capital over variable capital exceeding the social average) yields a lower than average rate of profit; capital with a "low organic composition" yields a higher than average rate of profit. The competition of capitals, and the freedom with which they transfer from one branch to another reduces the rate of profit to the average in both cases. The sum total of the values of all the commodities of a given society coincides with the sum total of prices of the commodities; but, owing to competition, in individual undertakings and branches of production commodities are sold not at their values but at the *prices of production* (or production prices), which are equal to the expended capital plus the average profit.

In this way the well-known and indisputable fact of

the divergence between prices and values and of the equalization of profits is fully explained by Marx on the basis of the law of value; for the total of values of all commodities coincides with the sum total of prices. However, the reduction of (social) value to (individual) prices does not take place simply and directly, but in a very complex way. It is quite natural that in a society of separate producers of commodities, who are united only by the market, law can reveal itself only as an average, social, mass law, when individual deviations to one side or the other mutually compensate one another.

An increase in the productivity of labor implies a more rapid growth of constant capital as compared with variable capital. And since surplus value is a function of variable capital alone, it is obvious that the rate of profit (the ratio of surplus value to the whole capital, and not to its variable part alone) tends to fall. Marx makes a detailed analysis of this tendency and of a number of circumstances that conceal or counteract it.

Without pausing to give an account of the extremely interesting sections of the third volume of *Capital* devoted to usurer's capital, commercial capital and money capital, we pass to the most important section, the theory of *ground rent*. Owing to the fact that the land area is limited and, in capitalist countries, is all occupied by individual private owners, the price of production of agricultural products is determined by the cost of production not on average soil, but on the worst soil, not under average conditions, but under the worst conditions of delivery of produce to the market. The difference between this price and the price of production on better soil (or under better conditions) constitutes *differential* rent. Analyzing this in detail, and showing how it arises out of the difference in fertility of different plots of land and the difference in the amount of capital invested in land, Marx fully exposed (see also *Theories of Surplus Value,* in which the criticism of Rodbertus deserves particular attention) the error of Ricardo, who considered that differential rent is derived only when there is a successive transition from better land to worse. On the contrary, there may be inverse transitions, land may pass from one category into others (owing to advances in agricultural technique, the growth of towns, and so on), and the notorious "law of diminishing returns" is a profound error which charges nature with the defects, limitations and contradictions of capitalism.

Further, the equalization of profit in all branches of industry and national economy in general presupposes complete freedom of competition and the free flow of capital from one branch to another. But the private ownership of land creates monopoly, which hinders this free flow. Owing to this monopoly, the products of agriculture, which is distinguished by a lower organic composition of capital, and, consequently, by an individually higher rate of profit, do not participate in the entirely free process of equalization of the rate of profit: the landowner, being a monopolist, can keep the price above the average, and this monopoly price engenders *absolute rent.*

Differential rent cannot be done away with under capitalism, but absolute rent *can*—for instance, by the nationalization of the land, by making it the property of the state. Making the land the property of the state would put an end to the monopoly of private landowners, and would lead to a more systematic and complete application of freedom of competition in the domain of agriculture. And, therefore, Marx points out, in the course of history bourgeois radicals have again and again advanced this progressive bourgeois demand for the nationalization of the land, which, however, frightens away the majority of the bourgeoisie, because it too closely "touches" another monopoly, which is particularly important and "sensitive" in our day—the monopoly of the means of production in general. (Marx gives a remarkably popular, concise, and clear exposition of his theory of the average rate of profit on capital and of absolute ground rent in a letter to Engels, dated August 2, 1862. See *Briefwechsel,* Vol III, pp. 77–81; also letter of August 9, 1862, pp. 86–87.)[26]

For this history of ground rent it is also important to note Marx's analysis showing how labor rent (when the peasant creates surplus product by laboring on the lord's land) is transformed into rent in produce or in kind (when the peasant creates surplus product on his own land and cedes it to the lord due to "non-economic constraint"), then into money rent (which is rent in kind transformed into money, the *obrok* [quit-rent] of old Russia, due to the development of commodity production, and finally into capitalist rent, when the peasant is replaced by the agricultural entrepreneur, who cultivates the soil with the help of wage-labor. In connection with this analysis of the "genesis of capitalist ground rent," note should be made of a number of subtle ideas (especially important for backward countries like Russia) expressed by Marx on the *evolution of capitalism in agriculture.*

"The transformation of rent in kind into money rent is not only necessarily accompanied, but even anticipated by the formation of a class of propertyless day laborers, who hire themselves out for wages. During the period of their rise, when this new class appears but sporadically, the custom necessarily develops among the better situated tributary farmers of exploiting agricultural laborers for their own account, just as the wealthier serfs in feudal times used to employ serfs for their own benefit. In this way they gradually acquire the ability to accumulate a certain amount of wealth and to transform themselves even into future capitalists. The old self-employing possessors of the land thus give rise among themselves to a nursery for capitalist tenants, whose development is conditioned upon the general development of capitalist production outside of the rural districts".[27]

"The expropriation and eviction of a part of the agricultural population not only set free for industrial capital, the laborers, their means of subsistence, and material for labor; it also created the home market."[28]

The impoverishment and ruin of the agricultural population lead, in their turn, to the formation of a reserve army of labor for capital. In every capitalist country "part of the agricultural population is therefore constantly on the point of passing over into an urban or manufacturing proletariat. . . . (Manufacture is used here in the sense of all non-agricultural industries.) This source of relative surplus population is thus constantly flowing. . . . The agricultural labor is therefore reduced to the minimum of wages, and always stands with one foot in the swamp of pauperism".[29]

The private ownership of the peasant in the land he tills constitutes the basis of small-scale production and the condition for its prospering and attaining a classical form. But such small-scale production is compatible only with a narrow and primitive framework of production and society. Under capitalism the "exploitation [of the peasants] differs only in *form* from the exploitation of the industrial proletariat. The exploiter is the same; *capital.* The individual capitalists exploit the individual peasants through *mortgages* and *usury;* the capitalist class exploits the peasant class through the state taxes".[30] "The small holding of the peasant is now only the pretext that allows the capitalist to draw profits, interest and rent from the soil, while leaving it to the tiller of the soil himself to see how he can extract his wages."[31] As a rule the peasant cedes to capitalist society, *i.e.,* to the capitalist class, even a part of the wages, sinking "to the level of the *Irish tenant farmer*—all under the pretense of being a *private proprietor".*[32]

What is "one of the causes which keeps the price of cereals lower in countries with a predominance of small farmers than in countries with a capitalist mode of production?" It is that the peasant cedes to society (i.e., to the capitalist class) part of his surplus product without an equivalent. "This lower price [of cereals and other agricultural produce] is also a result of the poverty of the producers and by no means of the productivity of labor." The smallholding system, which is the normal form of small-scale production, deteriorates, collapses, perishes under capitalism:

"Small peasants' property excludes by its very nature the development of the social powers of production of labor, the social forms of labor, the social concentration of capitals, cattle raising on a large scale, and a progressive application of science.

"Usury and a system of taxation must impoverish it everywhere. The expenditure of capital in the price of the land withdraws this capital from cultivation. An infinite dissipation of means of production and an isolation of the producers themselves go with it. [Co-operative societies, i.e., associations of small peasants, while playing an extremely progressive bourgeois role, only weaken this tendency without eliminating it; nor must it be forgotten that these co-operative societies do much for the well-to-do peasants, and very little, almost nothing, for the mass of poor peasants; and then the associations themselves become exploiters of wage-labor.] Also an enormous waste of human energy. A progressive deterioration of the conditions of production and a raising of the price of production is a necessary law of small peasants' property."[33]

In agriculture, as in industry, capitalism transforms the process of production only at the price of the "martyrdom of the producers."

"The dispersion of the rural laborers over larger areas breaks their power of resistance while concentration increases that of the town operatives. In modern agriculture, as in the urban industries, the increased productiveness and quantity of the labor set in motion are bought at the cost of laying waste and consuming by disease labor power itself. Moreover, all progress in capitalistic agriculture is a progress in the art, not only of robbing the laborer, but of robbing the soil. . . . Capitalist production, therefore, develops technology, and the combining together of various processes into a social whole, only by sapping the original sources of all wealth—the soil and the laborer".[34]

Socialism

From the foregoing it is evident that Marx induces the inevitability of the transformation of capitalist society into socialist society wholly and exclusively from the economic law of motion of contemporary society. The socialization of labor, which is advancing ever more rapidly in thousands of forms, and which has manifested itself very strikingly during the thirty years that has elapsed since the death of Marx in the growth of large-scale production, capitalist cartels, syndicates and trusts, as well as in the gigantic increase in the dimensions and power of finance capital, forms the chief material foundation for the inevitable coming of socialism. The intellectual and moral driving force and the physical executant of this transformation is the proletariat, which is trained by capitalism itself. The struggle of the proletariat against the bourgeoisie, which manifests itself in various and, as to its content, increasingly richer forms, inevitably becomes a political struggle aiming at the conquest of political power by the proletariat ("the dictatorship of the proletariat").

The socialization of production is bound to lead to the conversion of the means of production into the property of society, to the "expropriation of the expropriators." This conversion will result directly in an immense increase in productivity of labor, a reduction of working hours, and the replacement of the remnants, the ruins of small-scale primitive, disunited production by collective and improved labor. Capitalism finally snaps the bond between agriculture and industry; but at the same time, in its highest development it prepares new elements of this bond, of a union between industry and agriculture based on the conscious application of science and the combination of collective labor, and on a redistribution of the human population (putting an end at one and the same time to the rural remoteness, isolation and barbarism, and to the unnatural concentration of vast masses of people in big cities).

A new form of family, new conditions in the status of women and in the upbringing of the younger generation are being prepared by the higher forms of modern capitalism: female and child labor and the break-up of the patriarchal family by capitalism inevitably assume the most terrible, disastrous, and repulsive forms in modern society. Nevertheless "modern industry, by assigning as it does an important part in the process of production, outside the domestic sphere, to women, to young persons, and to children of both sexes, creates a new economical foundation for a higher form of the family and of the relations between the sexes. It is, of course, just as absurd to hold the Teutonic-Christian form of the family to be absolute and final as it would be to apply that character to the ancient Roman, the ancient Greek, or the Eastern forms which, moreover, taken together form a series in historic development. Moreover, it is obvious that the fact of the collective working group being composed of individuals of both sexes and all ages, must necessarily, under suitable conditions, become a source of humane development; although in its spontaneously developed, brutal, capitalistic form, where the laborer exists for the process of production, and not the process of production for the laborer, that fact is a pestiferous source of corruption and slavery". In the factory system is to be found "the germ of the education of the future, an education that will, in the case of every child over a given age, combine productive labor with instruction and gymnastics, not only as one of the methods of adding to the efficiency of production, but as the only method of producing fully developed human beings".[35]

Marxian Socialism put the question of nationality and of the state on the same historical footing, not only in the sense of explaining the past but also in the sense of a fearless forecast of the future and of bold practical action for its achievement. Nations are an inevitable product, an inevitable form in the bourgeois epoch of social development. The working class could not grow strong, could not become mature and formed without "constituting itself within the nation," without being "national" ("though not in the bourgeois sense of the word"). But the development of capitalism more and more breaks down national barriers, destroys national seclusions, substitutes class antagonisms for national antagonisms. It is, therefore, perfectly true that in the developed capitalist countries "the workingmen have no country" and that "united action" of the workers, of the civilized countries at least, "is one of the first conditions for the emancipation of the proletariat".[36]

The state, which is organized violence, inevitably came into being at a definite stage in the development of society, when society had split into irreconcilable classes, and when it could not exist without an "authority" ostensibly standing above society and to a certain degree separate from society. Arising out of class contradictions, the state becomes "the state of the most powerful economic class that by virtue of its economic supremacy becomes also the ruling political class, and so acquires new means of holding down and exploiting the oppressed class. The ancient state was, above all, the state of the slave-owners for holding down the slaves, just as the feudal state was the organ of the nobility for holding down the peasant serfs and bondsmen, and the modern representative state is the instrument for the exploitation of wage-labor by capital."[37]

Even the freest and most progressive form of the bourgeois state, the democratic republic, in no way removes this fact, but merely changes its form (connection between the government and the stock exchange, corruption—direct and indirect—of the officialdom and the press, etc.). Socialism, by leading to the abolition of classes, will thereby lead to the abolition of the state.

"The first act," writes Engels in *Anti-Dühring*, "in which the state really comes forward as the representative of society as a whole—the taking possession of the means of production in the name of society—is at the same time its last independent act as a state. The interference of the state power in social relations becomes superfluous in one sphere after another, and then ceases of itself. The government of persons is replaced by the administration of things and the direction of the processes of production. The state is 'abolished,' *it withers away.*"[38]

"The society organizes production anew on the basis of free and equal association of the producers which will put the whole state machinery where it will then belong—into the museum of antiquities, next to the spinning wheel and the bronze axe."[39]

Finally, as regards the attitude of Marxian Socialism towards the small peasanty, which will continue to exist in the period of the expropriation of the expropriators, we must refer to a declaration made by Engels which expresses Marx's views.

"When we take possession of the state power, we shall not even think of forcibly expropriating the small peasants (with or without compensation), as we shall have to do in relation to the large landowners. Our task as regards the small peasants will first of all be to lead their private enterprise and private property into co-operative lines, not forcibly, but by example and by granting public aid for this purpose. And then, of course, we shall have ample means of showing the small peasant all the advantages connected with such a transformation, advantages which even now should be explained to him" (Engels, "The Peasant Question in France and Germany." Original in the *Neue Zeit*).

Tactics of the Class Struggle of the Proletariat

Having as early as 1844–45 examined one of the chief defects of the earlier materialism,[39] namely, its inability to understand the conditions or appreciate the importance of practical-revolutionary activity, Marx, along with his theoretical work, all his life devoted constant attention to the tactical problems of the class struggle of the proletariat. An immense amount of material bearing on this is contained in *all* the works of Marx and particularly in the four volumes of his correspondence with Engels published in 1913. This material is still far from having been assembled, collated, studied and examined. We shall therefore have to confine ourselves here to the most general and briefest remarks, emphasizing that Marx justly considered that without *this* side to it materialism was irresolute, one-sided, and lifeless.

Marx defined the fundamental task of proletarian tactics in strict conformity with all the postulates of his materialist-dialectical conception. Only an objective consideration of the sum total of reciprocal relations of all the classes of a given society without exception, and, consequently, a consideration of the objective stage of development of that society and of the reciprocal relations between it and other societies, can serve as a basis for the correct tactics of the advanced class. At the same time, all classes and all countries are not regarded statically, but dynamically, i.e., not in a state of immobility, but in motion (the laws of which are determined by the economic conditions of existence of each class). Motion, in its turn, is regarded not only from the standpoint of the past, but also from the standpoint of the future, and, at the same time, not in accordance with the vulgar conception of the "evolutionists," who see only slow changes, but dialectically: in historical developments of such magnitude twenty years are no more than a day, Marx wrote to Engels, "although later there may come days in which twenty years are concentrated" (*Briefwechsel*, Vol. III, p. 127).[41] At each stage of development, at each moment, proletarian tactics must take account of this objectively inevitable dialectics of human history, on the one hand utilizing the periods of political stagnation or of sluggish, so-called "peaceful" development in order to develop the class consciousness, strength and fighting capacity of the advanced class, and, on the other hand, conducting all this work of utilization towards the "final aim" of the movement of the advanced class and towards the creation in it of the faculty for practically performing great tasks in the great days in which "twenty years are concentrated."

Two of Marx's arguments are of special importance in this connection: one of these is contained in *The Poverty of Philosophy* and concerns the economic struggle and economic organizations of the proletariat; the other is contained in the *Communist Manifesto* and concerns the political tasks of the proletariat. The first argument runs as follows:

"Large-scale industry concentrates in one place a crowd of people unknown to one another. Competition divides their interests. But the maintenance of wages, this common interest which they have against their boss, unites them in a common thought of resistance—*combination*. . . . Combinations, at first isolated, constitute themselves into groups . . . and in face of always united capital, the maintenance of the association becomes more necessary to them [i.e., the workers] than that of wages. . . . In this struggle—a veritable civil war—are united and developed all the elements necessary for a coming battle. Once it has reached this point, association takes on a political character."[42]

Here we have the program and tactics of the economic struggle and of the trade union movement for several decades to come, for the whole long period in which the proletariat will muster its forces for the "coming battle." Side by side with this must be placed numerous references by Marx and Engels to the example of the British labor movement: how industrial "prosperity" leads to attempts "to buy the workers" (*Briefwechsel*, Vol. I, p. 136), to divert them from the struggle; how this prosperity generally "demoralizes the workers" (Vol. II, p. 213); how the British proletariat becomes "bourgeoisified"—"this most bourgeois of all nations seems to want in the end to have a bourgeois aristocracy and a bourgeois proletariat side by side with the bourgeoisie" (Vol. II, p. 290); how its "revolutionary energy" oozes away (Vol. III, p. 124), how it will be necessary to wait a more or less long time "before the British workers rid themselves of their apparent bourgeois corruption" (Vol. III, p. 127); how the British labor movement "lacks the mettle of the Chartists" (1866; Vol. III, p. 305); how the British workers' leaders are becoming a type midway between "a radical bourgeois and a worker" (in reference to Holyoake, Vol. IV, p. 209); how, owing to British monopoly, and as long as this monopoly lasts, "the British workingman will not budge" (Vol. IV, p. 433). The tactics of the economic struggle, in connection with the general course (*and outcome*) of the labor movement, are here considered from a remarkably broad, comprehensive, dialectical, and genuinely revolutionary standpoint.

The *Communist Manifesto* set forth the fundamental Marxian principle on the tactics of the political struggle: "The Communists fight for the attainment of the immediate aims, for the enforcement of the momentary interests of the working class; but in the movement of the present, they also represent and take care of the future of that movement."[43]

That was why in 1848 Marx supported the party of the "agrarian revolution" in Poland, "the party which initiated the Cracow insurrection in the year 1846." In Germany in 1848 and 1849 Marx supported the extreme revolutionary democracy, and subsequently never retracted what he had then said about tactics. He regarded the German bourgeoisie as an element which "was inclined from the very beginning to betray the people" (only an alliance with the peasantry could have brought the bourgeoisie the integral fulfillment of its aims) "and to compromise with the crowned representatives of the old society." Here is Marx's summary of the analysis of the class position of the German bourgeoisie in the era of the bourgeois-democratic revolution—an analysis which, incidentally, is a sample of that materialism which examines society in motion, and examines it, at the same time, not only from the side of the motion which is directed *backwards!*

"Lacking faith in itself, lacking faith in the people, grumbling at those above, trembling before those below . . . intimidated by the world storm . . . nowhere with energy, everywhere with plagiarism . . . without initiative . . . an execrable old man, doomed to guide the first youthful impulses of a youthful and robust people in his own senile interests . . . " (*Neue Rheinische Zeitung*, 1848; see *Literarischer Nachlass*, Vol. III, p. 212).

About twenty years later, in a letter to Engels (*Briefwechsel*, Vol. III, p. 224), Marx declared that the cause of the failure of the Revolution of 1848 was that the bourgeoisie had preferred peace with slavery to the mere prospect of a fight for freedom. When the revolutionary era of 1848–49 ended, Marx opposed every attempt to play at revolution (the fight he put up against Schapper and Willich), and insisted on the ability to work in the new phase that in a seemingly "peaceful" way was preparing for new revolutions. The spirit in which Marx wanted the work to be carried on is shown by his estimate of the situation in Germany in 1856, the blackest period of reaction: "The whole thing in Germany will depend on the possibility to back the proletarian revolution by some second edition of the Peasant War" (*Briefwechsel*, Vol. II, p. 108).

As long as the democratic (bourgeois) revolution in Germany was not finished, Marx wholly concentrated attention in the tactics of the Socialist proletariat on developing the democratic energy of the peasantry. He held that Lassalle's attitude was "objectively . . . a betrayal of the whole workers' movement to Prussia" (*Briefwechsel,* Vol. III, p. 210), incidentally because Lassalle connived at the actions of the Junkers and Prussian nationalism.

"In a predominantly agricultural country," wrote Engels in 1865, exchanging ideas with Marx on the subject of an intended joint statement by them in the press, " . . . it is dastardly . . . in the name of the industrial proletariat to attack the bourgeoisie exclusively, and never to say a word about the patriarchal cudgel exploitation of the rural proletariat by the big feudal nobles" (*Briefwechsel,* Vol. III, p. 217).

From 1864 to 1870, when the era of the completion of the bourgeois-democratic revolution in Germany, the era of the efforts of the exploiting classes of Prussia and Austria to complete this revolution in one way or another *from above,* was coming to an end, Marx not only condemned Lassalle, who was coquetting with Bismarck, but also corrected Liebknecht, who had inclined towards "Austrophilism" and the defense of particularism.[44] Marx demanded revolutionary tactics which would combat both Bismarck and the Austrophiles with equal ruthlessness, tactics which would not be adapted to the "victor," the Prussian Junker, but which would immediately renew the revolutionary struggle against him *also on the basis* created by the Prussian military victories (*Briefwechsel,* Vol. III, p. 134, 136, 147, 179, 204, 210, 215, 418, 437, 440–41).

In the famous Address[45] of the International Working Men's Association of September 9, 1870, Marx warned the French proletariat against an untimely uprising; but when the uprising nevertheless took place (1871), Marx enthusiastically hailed the revolutionary initiative of the masses, who were "storming heaven" (letter of Marx to Kugelmann).[46] The defeat of the revolutionary action in this situation, as in many others, was, from the standpoint of Marxian dialectical materialism, a lesser evil in the general course *and outcome* of the proletarian struggle than the abandonment of a position already occupied, than a surrender without battle. Such a surrender would have demoralized the proletariat and undermined its fighting capacity. Fully appreciating the use of legal means of struggle during periods when political stagnation prevails and bourgeois legality dominates, Marx, in 1877 and 1878, after the passage of the Anti-Socialist Law,[47] sharply condemned Most's "revolutionary phrases"; but he no less, if not more sharply, attacked the opportunism that had temporarily gained sway in the official Social-Democratic Party, which did not at once display resoluteness, firmness, revolutionary spirit and a readiness to resort to an illegal struggle in response to the Anti-Socialist Law (*Briefwechsel*, Vol. IV, p. 397, 404, 418, 422, 424; *see* also letters to Sorge[48]).

July-November 1914

9. SPEECH AT THE UNVEILING OF A MONUMENT TO MARX AND ENGELS ON NOVEMBER 7, 1918*

WE are unveiling a memorial to the leaders of the world workers' revolution, to Marx and Engels.

Humanity suffered and languished for ages under the oppression of a tiny handful of exploiters who tortured millions of toilers. But while the exploiters of the previous epoch, the landlords, robbed and pressed down the peasants, the serfs, who were disunited, scattered and ignorant, the exploiters of the new period saw before them, among the down-trodden masses, the vanguard of these masses: the industrial factory workers of the towns. The factory united them, town life enlightened them, the common struggle in strikes as well as revolutionary action hardened them.

The great world-wide historical service of Marx and Engels lies in the fact that they proved by scientific analysis the inevitability of the downfall of capitalism and its transition to communism under which there will be no more exploitation of man by man.

See Lenin, *Collected Works*, English edition, 28:165–66

The great world-wide historical service of Marx and Engels lies in this, that they indicated to the proletarians of all countries their role, their task, their calling: to be the first to rise in the revolutionary fight against capital and unite around themselves in this struggle *all* the toilers and the exploited.

We are living in a happy time, when the forecast of the great socialists is beginning to come true. We all see the dawn of the international socialist revolution in a whole number of countries. The unspeakable horrors of the imperialist butchery of the peoples are evoking the heroic upsurge of the oppressed masses, and are increasing their forces tenfold in the struggle for emancipation.

May the monument to Marx and Engels remind the millions of workers and peasants that we do not stand alone in the struggle. The workers of the more advanced countries are rising side by side with us. Hard battles are still in store for them and ourselves. The yoke of capital will be broken in the common struggle and Socialism will finally triumph!

REFERENCE NOTES

Frederick Engels

1. Lenin wrote *Frederick Engels* in the autumn of 1895. It was first published in March 1896 in the symposium *Rabotnik*, No. 1. *Rabotnik (The Worker)* was published abroad from 1896–1899 by the League of Russian Social-Democrats. On April 25 (May 7), 1895, Lenin went abroad to establish contacts with the Emancipation of Labour group and to study the West European workers' movement. Lenin initiated the publication of *Rabotnik*, reaching agreement with G. V. Plekhanov, P. B. Axelrod and other members of the group. On returning to Russia in September 1895, Lenin made every effort to provide *Rabotnik* with articles and correspondence from Russia and to organize financial support for it. Lenin wrote several other items in addition to "Frederick Engels" for the first issue. All in all, six issues of *Rabotnik* were published in three volumes, and ten issues of *Listok Rabotnika (The Workers' Newssheet)*.
2. The words are from a poem by N. A. Nekrasov, "In Memory of Dobrolyubov."
3. See n.1, above.
4. Engels's preface to the Second Edition, *The Peasant War in Germany*, New York (1966), p.27.
5. *The German-French Annuals*, journal founded by Marx jointly with A. Ruge in Paris. Only one issue of it (double) appeared in 1844. Marx was banished from Paris in 1845.
6. Lenin refers to *Anti-Dühring* by Engels.
7. A literary and political review published abroad in 1890–1892 by the Emancipation of Labour group; just four issues appeared. Lenin refers to Engels's article "Foreign Policy of Russian Tsarism."
8. Refers to Engels, *The Housing Question*, written in 1872–1873 and revised by Engels in 1887.
9. Engels, "On Social Relations in Russia," written in April 1875 and published in *Volksstaat* that year, as well as a separate pamphlet in 1875 and 1894. Available in some editions of Marx/Engels *Selected Works*.
10. Refers to *Theories of Surplus Value*, to appear in full along with

Capital in the *Marx/Engels Collected Works*, Vols. 30–34. No longer considered as Volume IV of *Capital*, but in fact as work that pre-dated *Capital.*
11. Engels's letter to J. F. Becker, October 15, 1884.

Our Program

1. One of the articles Lenin wrote during his exile in 1899, intended for *Rabochaya Gazeta*, which had been adopted as the official organ of the R.S.D.L.P. at its First Congress. However, renewal of publication was unsuccessful and Lenin's articles were not published. See V. I. Lenin, *Collected Works*, Vol. 4.
2. Refers to Plekhanov's article, "Bernstein and Materialism," published in No. 44 of *Neue Zeit (New Times)*, organ of the German Social-Democrats, July, 1898.
3. The Hannover Congress of the German Social-Democrats was held from September 27 to October 2 (October 9–14), 1899. In the discussion of the chief point on the agenda, "The Attack on the Fundamental Views and Tactics of the Party," the Congress voted against Bernstein's revisionist views, without, however, subjecting them to an extensive criticism.
4. (*Workers' Thought*), organ of the opportunist Economists, was published in 16 issues from October 1897 to December 1902. Lenin's *Iskra* was an important instrument against the ideas of economism, but Lenin's most complete response is in *What Is To Be Done?*
5. The law of June 2 (14), 1897 established an 11-1/2 hour workday for industrial and railway shops. Prior to this the working day in Russia had been as long as 14 or 15 hours. Pressure from the working-class movement, including strikes, headed by the League of Struggle for the Emancipation of the Working Class under Leninist leadership forced the czarist government to issue the June law.
6. The *Manifesto* of the R.S.D.L.P. was published in 1898, on the instructions of the First Congress, by the Central Committee of the R.S.D.L.P. The Manifesto advanced the struggle for political freedom and the overthrow of the autocracy to the forefront of the Russian Social-Democratic movement, and linked the political struggle with the general objectives of the working-class movement.

Engels on Theoretical Struggle

1. Excerpt from Lenin, *What Is To Be Done?*, New York (1969), pp. 25–29
2. Letter from Karl Marx to W. Bracke, May 1875. Text is in Marx/Engels *Selected Works* (In One Volume), New York, p. 317.
3. See *Peasant War in Germany*, New York (1966), pp. 27–30

Differences in the European Labour Movement

1. See Lenin, *Collected Works* 16: 347–52. The article "*Differences in the European Labour Movement*" was published in No. 1 of the newspaper *Zvezda* (*The Star*), in the section entitled "Letters from Abroad".

   Zvezda—a Bolshevik legal newspaper, the predecessor of *Pravda*; it was issued in St. Petersburg from December 16 (29), 1910 to April 22 (May 5), 1912 On February 26 (March 10), 1912, there appeared simultaneously with *Zvezda* the first issue of *Nevskaya Zvezda*, which became the continuation of *Zvezda* after the latter had been closed down. The last, 27th, issue of *Nevskaya Zvezda* was published on October 5 (18), 1912. Until the autumn of 1911, pro-Party Mensheviks (Plekhanovites) participated in *Zvezda*. The ideological leadership of the newspaper was carried out (from abroad) by Lenin, who published in it and in *Nevskaya Zvezda* about 50 articles.

   The legal newspaper *Zvezda* directed by Lenin was a militant Bolshevik organ which upheld the programme of the illegal Party. *Zvezda* established permanent close ties with the workers and devoted an extensive section to workers' correspondence. The circulation of individual issues reached 50,000–60,000. The newspaper suffered continual persecution by the government; out of 96 issues of *Zvezda* and *Nevskaya Zvezda*, 39 were confiscated and 10 were subjected to fines. *Zvezda* prepared the way for the publication of the Bolshevik daily newspaper *Pravda* and was closed down on the day that *Pravda* appeared. p. 347
2. The "*Young*" faction—a petty-bourgeois semi-anarchist group formed in the German Social-Democratic Party in 1890 and composed chiefly of undergraduate students and young writers (hence the name). It put forward a platform that rejected

any Social-Democratic participation in parliament. They were expelled from the Party by the Erfurt Congress in October 1891.   p. 351

3. *Johann Most*—German Social-Democrat. In 1880, at the Baden Congress, he was expelled from the Party on account of his disorganising behaviour. In the eighties he became an adherent of anarchism. Most arrived in the United States in 1882 and quickly became a leader of U.S. anarchists, favoring individual terrorist acts and holding political action to be useless, as well as downgrading trade union work.

Certain Features of the Historical Development of Marxism (December, 1910).

1. *Vekhi (Landmarks)* was a symposium published in Moscow in the spring of 1909, containing articles by N. Berdyaev, S. Bulgakov, P. Struve and other liberal-monarchist bourgeois writers who opposed the revolutionary movement and urged the intelligentsia to serve the autocracy. Lenin called the symposium an "encyclopedia of liberal renegacy."

2. Lenin is here referring to the influence of Ernst Mach (1838–1916), Austrian physicist, psychologist and philosopher who was the leading figure of the new "positivism" known as "empirio-criticism." Lenin wrote his major philosophical work, *Materialism and Empirio-Criticism* in 1908 to combat the Machist and similar tendencies in Marxist circles.

3. *Otzovism* (from the Russian word *otzovat*—to recall) was an opportunist trend among a small section of the Bolsheviks which arose after the defeat of the Revolution of 1905–07. The group demanded the recall of the Social-Democratic deputies from the State Duma, non-participation in parliamentary elections, and rejection of work in the trade unions and other mass organizations.

The Three Sources and Three Component Parts of Marxism

1. Lenin wrote this article on the 30th Anniversary of the death of Marx (March 1913).

Historical Destiny of the Doctrine of Karl Marx (March 1913).

1. *Narodism*, literally "populism," is the term first applied to the social movement of the 'sixties of the last century in Russia. Its most characteristic feature was the belief in the possibility of non-capitalist development of Russia and the attainment of socialism without the working class and on the basis of the village commune.

Karl Marx

1. Frederick Engels, *Ludwig Feuerbach* (written in 1880s), New York, 1941, p.18.
2. For the bibliography, see Lenin, *Collected Works 21*: p.80.
3. See Marx/Engels *Collected Works* (hereinafter referred to as M/E *CW*) 3:175–87; 229–346; 418–43. Engels's *Outlines of a Critique of Political Economy* is also in the appendix of Marx, *Economic and Philosophic Manuscripts of 1844*, ed. by Dirk Struik, New York, 1964.
4. M/E *CW* 4:5–211, "The Holy Family"; 5:3–8,"Theses on Feuerbach"; 5:19–581, "The Poverty of Philosophy"; 6:105–12, "Wage-Labour and Capital"; 9:197–228, "Speech on the Question of Free Trade." (Writings of Marx and Engels on Malthus and on religion, 1844–48, are found in *CW* volumes 3–9.)
5. Karl Vogt (1817–95), a German democrat against whom Marx waged a polemic, exposing his connection with Napoleon III, in a book entitled *Herr Vogt*. See *CW* 17:21–329.
6. During this period Marx, with assistance from Engels, wrote frequently for the *New-York Tribune*, at the request of its managing editor (later editor), Charles A. Dana. Many of these articles have been reprinted in separate collections. See M/E *CW*, beginning with Volume 11 and succeeding volumes for the period 1851–1862.
7. The Inaugural Address and documents pertaining to the founding of the International Working Men's Association can be found in the M/E *CW*, vols. 20 and 21.
8. See n10, p. 83.
9. *Capital*, Afterword to the 2nd German edition.
10. Engels, *Anti-Dühring*, New York, 1939, pp. 50–51; 68;

42–43; 30. See also a famous excerpt from this work, *Socialism, Utopian and Scientific*, New York, 1935.

11. Engels, *Ludwig Fueurbach*, pp. 20–21.
12. ibid., p. 23
13. Engels, *Anti-Duhring*, p. 125.
14. Ibid, pp. 15; 29.
15. *Fueurbach*, pp. 44–45; 12
16. *Anti-Duhring*, p. 31.
17. *Fueurbach*, p. 29
18. *Capital I*: see long footnote near beginning of Chap. 15.
19. Selsam and Martel, eds., *Reader in Marxist Philosophy*, New York, 1963, pp. 186–87. The July 7, 1866, letter to Engels can be found in various volumes of M/E selected correspondence and the corresponding volume of M/E *CW* correspondence.
20. M/E *CW* 6:482; or *The Communist Manifesto*, New York, 1948, p. 9.
21. ibid., *CW* 494; p. 19
22. *Capital I*, chap. 1, section 1, "Commodities"
23. ibid., chap. 6.
24. ibid.
25. ibid., chap. 32
26. Letters in various volumes of M/E correspondence and in corresponding M/E *CW*. Lenin's references are to the German editions. See *CW* 41:394, 403.
27. *Capital III*: chap. 47, part iv "Money rent"
28. *Capital I*: chap. 30
29. ibid., chap. 25, section 4
30. Marx, *Class Struggles in France*, New York, 1964, pp. 119–20. M/E *CW* 10: 121–22
31. Marx, *The 18th Brumaire of Louis Bonaparte*, New York, 1963, p. 127. M/E *CW* 11: 190
32. *Class Struggles in France*, p. 119; M/E *CW* 10: 121
33. *Capital III*: chap. 47, section 5
34. *Capital I*: chap. 15, section 10
35. ibid., section 9
36. *Communist Manifesto*, p. 28; M/E *CW* 6:502–3
37. Engels, *Origin of the Family*, New York, 1972, p. 231
38. *Anti-Duhring*, p. 407
39. *Origin of the Family*, p. 232
40. Lenin is referring to M/E, "The Holy Family,"(*CW* 4:5–11); "The German Ideology," (*CW* 5:19–539); Marx, "Theses on

Fueurbach," (*CW* 5:3–9); also found as an appendix in Engels *Ludwig Fueurbach.*

41. M/E letters of the 1860s. See n26 above.
42. Marx, *The Poverty of Philosophy*, New York, 1963, pp. 172–73. Also M/E *CW* 6:210:11.
43. The *Manifesto*, p. 43; *CW* 6:518
44. See M/E *CW* 20–21 and corresponding volumes of the correspondence. For a later criticism by Marx, see *Critique of the Gotha Programme*, New York, 1966.
45. Marx, *The Civil War in France*, New York, 1968, pp. 28–35; M/E *CW*:22
46. Marx, *Letters to Kugelman*, New York, 1934, letter of April 12, 1871, p. 123.
47. The Anti-Socialist Law was introduced in Germany in 1878. The Law banned all organizations of the Social-Democratic Party, the workers' mass organizations, and the labor press; Socialist listerature was confiscated, and Social-Democrats were exiled. It was abrogated in 1890 under pressure of the mass labor movement.
48. Many of these letters can be found in Marx and Engels, *Letters to Americans, 1848–1895*, New York, 1953; also in volumes of correspondence, M/E *CW.*